D1057924

"Nathan has done it again! *Serve Up, Coach Down* clearly outlines what all leaders should be doing regardless of their position. The real examples coupled with the specific actions to take, make these concepts easy to implement. *The Sales Leaders Playbook* is required reading for my directors and since implementing those ideas, I have seen a significant improvement in our results. This is another of Nathan's books that will be required reading for all my directors, and I expect us to reach another level with these insights!"

—Darren Howden, senior vice president, Prairie Operations, Farm Credit Canada

"This book is a great tool for anyone in management, at any stage of their career, to learn how to achieve success and fulfilment with a fresh perspective on 360 degrees workplace relationships with their the boss, employees, peers and customers. The simple situational examples and recommendations offered clear explanations and strategies for managers to follow for improved relationships and performance in their careers. As a sales leader for over twenty-five years in a service industry, I almost felt as though your examples and recommendations came right from the realities from best practices in my business and career. Thanks for SERVING this book for me & others to read!"

—Ken Bisnoff, founding executive, TPx Communications

"If you lead people and answer to someone, this book is for you. Become more of the leader your boss and team respects! This book will teach you about what servant leadership should mean, serving up to the boss and serving out to peers and down by coaching. This true mindset shift will empower and hold the entire team accountable to exceed the wildest goals; often requiring difficult choices and doing things differently."

—Mike Leathers, president, TPG Pressure Pipe Group

"Nathan Jamail does it again by providing a practical yet insightful and fresh way to approach leadership. The idea of serving up and coaching down truly puts you (and me) in a position of greater influence and power within our organizations. I've already tasked my team to allow their teams to 'run', and coach them to excellence. Nathan's methods can and should be applied to all business practices . . . large, small, private, public or non-profit."

—Michael Mabry, president,
Mooyah Burgers Fries & Shakes

"I loved this book. In today's business climate working together is critical. Your description of the mindset necessary to move a business plan or goal forward is spot on for any team, group, or workforce. I also thought the mindset of *Serve Up, Coach Down* was so true. This a book every leader and employee needs to read."

—Dan Murr, JMT Management

"Nathan's *Serve Up, Coach Down* principles kicks down the doors on the conventional wisdom of servant leadership. Nathan not only shows the value of being a servant to those you follow and a great coach to those you lead. He shows the true power of the Leader in the middle. This is a must read for any leader in business today!"

—Steve Peters, president, 20/20 Communications

SERVE UP

UP

MASTERING THE MIDDLE AND BOTH SIDES OF LEADERSHIP

COACH

DOWN

NATHAN JAMAIL

This edition first published in 2018 by Career Press,
an imprint of Red Wheel/Weiser, LLC
With offices at:
65 Parker Street, Suite 7
Newburyport, MA 01950
www.redwheelweiser.com
www.careerpress.com

ISBN: 978-1-63265-149-5
Library of Congress Cataloging-in-Publication Data
available upon request

Cover design by Kathryn Sky-Peck
Interior by Gina Schenck
Typeset in Minion Pro and Optima

Printed in the United States of America
LB
10 9 8 7 6 5 4 3 2 1

To you, the reader, the leader that serves up and coaches down. The leader who inspires those around them to be better by being selfless and committed.

ACKNOWLEDGMENTS

I want to thank God for allowing me to do what I love and aligning my passion with the gift I have been given. I want to thank my wife, cowriter, best friend, and super mother, Shannon; without her I would not be as blessed as I am today. My three daughters Nyla, Paige, and Savannah who every day remind Shannon and I just how blessed we are. My son Anthony, who this year will be a father himself and will understand a father's love for the first time.

Of course, my entire family: Mom, Dad, and brothers for giving me the gift of family and love. I also would like to thank Jim Eber for doing what he does and working his magic on this book. I am always amazed with how he can take my writing and stories and make them come alive.

Thank you to Megan Close for believing in the book and helping us connect with Career

Press. When I started this book, I did not know exactly what the words or the stories were going to be, but I knew my intent and my goal. My intent was to write a book that would truly help leaders, a book that would be used and read for decades to come. My goal was to write a book that could truly change and benefit any organization—not just from the top down or bottom up but from the middle out!

Lastly, I want to thank all of the great leaders whom I have been fortunate enough to work with and learn from over the many years. As I say in many of my speeches, I am the luckiest, most blessed person in world. Know that I may not be worthy, but I am eternally grateful.

Thank you for reading my book.

Contents

The Leader in the Middle

One of the most difficult leadership positions in business today is also the most common: the "leader in the middle." Leading from the middle simply means you lead a team (sometimes many teams of hundreds of people) and simultaneously report to someone as your boss. And how many people do you know who do not answer to *anyone*? It doesn't matter what their titles are: vice president, senior account executive, manager, director . . . It doesn't matter if they work for a Fortune 500, mid-market company, university, hospital, construction firm . . . It doesn't matter if they're part of a high-technology business in the cloud or legacy brick-and-mortar analog brand.

Simply put, if you lead people and answer to someone—a boss, shareholders, customers—you are among the millions of "leaders in the middle" in business today. Yet too few of those leaders have really figured out how to own the power that comes with that position.

Wait, Nathan, did you just say leading from the middle is *powerful?* Yes, I did.

Too many leaders don't see it that way. They think the middle is weak, lacks influence, and makes them ineffective at driving change. They feel it's an insult to be called "middle management." They treat the *M* like some leadership scarlet letter. But leading from the middle is not a judgment that you must hide from others in shame, and it's most certainly not weak. In fact, those who have mastered the middle are superstars that their bosses are grateful for, employees admire, peers respect, slackers fear, and victims resent. They lead through uncertainty and move at the speed of change that organizations need today.

Those who have failed to master the middle struggle to lead their people relentlessly to achieve success and simultaneously accept direction from their bosses. To solve this problem, what leaders and organizations need is a new approach that changes how they think about leading from the middle. How they prepare. How they execute.

Why do leaders in the middle who care about their teams still struggle to gain their boss's approval? Why do leaders in the middle who feel they serve their teams have so much difficulty getting teams to step it up and go beyond their basic requirements of their jobs? Why do leaders in the middle have issues working with other teams and divisions in the organization, leaving their teams having to do more work?

Because those leaders in the middle too often serve down to their people and defend up to their bosses, instead of serving up to their bosses and coaching down to their employees.

How Did This Happen?

The way most leaders have been taught, trained, and conditioned to lead, serve, and follow is not only misdirected but has hindered their paths to greater success, innovation, and creating cultures filled with stronger, happier employees. The solution to this problem, however, isn't to change direction; it's to shift our mindsets about what it means to serve.

Ever since Robert Greenleaf coined the term "servant leadership" in 1970, countless books have touted it as *the* way to lead. Invert the traditional hierarchical corporate pyramid and put the leaders at the bottom! Put others first and allow them to influence you! Serve your people! These are noble concepts but flawed in their execution. This is why after years of leadership development and practicing the idea of servant leadership, organizations still struggle to hold their people accountable, lead and execute through change, and align the needs and goals from the top to the bottom. This is also why leaders in the middle struggle to implement servant leadership, why companies struggle to find those leaders, and why traditional approaches too often fail in the long run.

Simply put, leaders in the middle must be willing to *serve up* to those they answer to, but to serve those they lead they must *coach down.*

We serve *up* to those we follow by: believing in them, following their directions, and working for the greater good of the organization.

We coach *down* to serve those we lead by: focusing on making them better, demanding they believe in themselves, and expecting they achieve greatness by becoming the best versions of themselves.

Yes, leaders should care about their people and allow them greater influence. But what good are leaders—and how much are they really able to care for their people—if they take the idea of serving people literally? Great leaders don't feed their people fish; they coach them on how to fish for themselves and then kick every competitor's ass by catching more of them. Those people in return serve those leaders and the people those leaders serve by delivering maximum performance for the organization.

We Need a New Playbook for Success

Achieving this level of performance requires leaders in the middle to focus, have confidence, and commit to changing their mindsets. That's what this book helps you do: realize your power by shifting your mindset to embrace the power of the middle by striking the necessary balance between coaching those you lead and serving those who lead you. When you understand the influence and impact you can have by serving up and coaching down, everyone wins, and you realize the power you have as a leader in the middle. You become more successful—better, faster, and stronger as a leader in the middle simply by shifting to a serve up/coach down mindset and doing things a little differently than you've been taught.

Put aside traditional notions of servant leadership and learn to serve up to your bosses, serve out to your peers, and coach down to those you lead with humility, selflessness, and confidence. It's time to change the way we lead from the middle by *transforming it* and *owning it* as a difficult, underappreciated, and more powerful position than we have ever realized.

PART 1

Serving Up

Let's say a person important to you was spending the night at your home. How would you treat that person when he or she arrived? With open arms, a big welcome, and a genuine smile or a half-hearted wave, a low grunt, and a half-assed gesture to where the guest room is? Would you offer a drink from the good stuff in a nice glass or some tap water from your kid's chewed-up sippy cup? Would you put clean sheets on the bed and set out the nice towels? Or would you leave the sheets Aunt Agnes with the pack-a-day habit slept on last week and put the frayed towels your dog likes to play with on top?

Most of us would not give a second thought to giving and serving our guest the best to make that person feel special and welcomed.

But what if that guest were our boss? Same thing, of course.

So let me ask you these questions: *Why is it okay to serve people who come to your home as guests but unacceptable to serve people who employ you and help you pay for that home? Why would you strive to be the best servant at home but think that doing the same thing at work is wrong or just sucking up?*

Because you lack the "serve up" mindset.

Chapter 1

Serve Your Boss and You Serve Your Team

"Nathan, I'm going to meet with my boss to let him know that my team cannot succeed with only three managers. I used to have four, as you know, but they never let me fill the position when Lisa left. It's just too much for us, man."

I could feel the tension through the phone in Steve's voice. Steve is the director of eight regional rehabilitation centers in California. He's good at his job and a well-liked and even respected leader, especially by his boss. But the stress was getting to him: After Lisa left for another job, the company decided to try and reorganize instead of filling her position. Steve's boss told him the team would have do the work with three managers for the time being.

Did you restructure the team and responsibilities like your boss asked?

"Who has time for that? You know I told him two weeks ago about how I stepped in to do some of Lisa's work in order to keep the team focused, and as a result, I don't have time for my director responsibilities."

But your responsibility is to be a director, not a manager. What have you asked of your team?

"Asked? Nothing. They were already overworked. I'm willing to put my job on the line for my demands. We need another manager for us to be successful."

Steve paused for a moment, but I said nothing. Cue awkward silence. Maybe he was expecting encouragement for his willingness to stand up to his boss for his team and himself. But if Steve was expecting praise from me, he was mistaken. What Steve was saying might have sounded good to him, but it was a terrible idea.

He finally broke the silence: "I'm going to do it, Nathan."

I pounced: *Don't you dare. If I were your boss and you told me this, I would be looking to replace you.*

"What? Why would you say that?"

You haven't put a plan in place and even tried to make it work with three managers. You haven't acted on what the boss told you to do, but you're acting like you failed. You've done nothing but allow your fear of what you think will happen determine your actions.

"But . . . I need to protect my team."

That's the fear talking. You say your team can't handle any more work—that they are already spread too thin, but you didn't demand anything from them to empower them. You defended and protected them. You even stepped in to perform some of the tasks. All because you think you know this can't be done—that if you give them more work, they might quit. But you don't know anything. Think about that.

Steve promised he would think about it. I hoped he would. He had a chance to learn perhaps the essential skill for leading from the middle: understanding what it means to serve up so you can serve your people by coaching down.

Defending Up Versus Demanding Down

Why was I so hard on Steve? It may seem that he was being a selfless and strong leader by standing up for his team to his boss and the company. He was serving his people by defending and protecting them, right? Wrong. Steve did the exact opposite of what he needed to do to make his team more successful, his boss more confident in his leadership, and him a powerful leader in the middle: *He defended up and protected down instead of demanding down and serving up.*

Defending up and protecting down—exemplified in this case by Steve trying to make his boss understand that his team was doing its best but was overworked—is a fatalist and a warped leadership mindset. We do a disservice to our people by serving them the same way we do our leaders, because what that usually leads to is serving down, *not* serving up. While Steve *thought* he was serving his people, he needed to *demand down to serve up.*

Serving up is how leaders in the middle exceed the expectations given by their bosses and the organization, deliver the best results, and demand more from their teams.

Coaching down is how leaders in the middle serve their teams, demanding more and empowering the people on those teams to serve their leaders and the organizations, while pushing them to exceed all expectations.

Your people don't need protection from your boss or your boss's bosses. Your people need leaders who believe in them. Who know they can thrive when faced with difficult challenges and setbacks. Who want to build on their successes. Who yearn to have a mission and a purpose.

When you defend your team, you are taking all that away. You are telling your people *and* those who they report to that the team (and you) are weak and incapable or unwilling to do more. Strong leaders in the middle know demanding and defending are contradictory actions, so they choose to demand down. They know the more their people are challenged and pushed, the more they achieve. And to do that genuinely and authentically requires a serve up mindset.

Stop Protecting Down

Steve's issue with his boss and company was based on headcount and fear that the reorganization would be too much work for his team. Did it matter that his boss and the company believed the work could be reorganized and done without the fourth manager? No. He wanted to maintain the status quo, and the status quo told him it was impossible before he even implemented it. So he defended up instead of serving up.

Steve needed to stop seeing his managers as over-worked, taken advantage of, unappreciated, and in need of protection. He needed to let the team members know that they were capable of doing more. He needed to push them to be better. Instead, despite all the countless studies that show failure is often productive to learning and growth,

Steve feared and anticipated failure and sought to avoid it before it even happened.

This is exactly what Steve did in the months that followed: He shifted his mindset from defending up to demanding down. He realized he could not solve his manager's problems. In fact, he might even have created and enabled them himself. By protecting them, he had become unengaged and unaware of their strengths and limitations. He stepped back and took a hard look at his three remaining managers and what the team needed to do to serve the company: reduce overall cost and increase efficiency.

When he did, he discovered that the issue was not the lack of a fourth manager, rather the lack of success of his current three. He realized his strongest manager was capable of much more, the second manager lacked the professional development necessary to deliver what he was capable of, and the weakest manager was likely in the wrong job and causing the team entire team to struggle. So he put the strongest manager in charge of all the clinics, took the time to develop one manager and saw great improvement, and moved the weakest manager to a new role that better aligned with her skills as he looked to hire a new manager that could take the team to the next level. As a result, Steve not only has gotten more out of his team by demanding down but also gotten more out of himself.

Will Steve's success lead to the results the company expects? He's turned himself and his expectations of his team around, but can he sustain it? That remains to be seen. Not all turnarounds end in increased profits and happier employees. Sometimes success is just measured in the awareness of the issues that a leader is unaware of. And I'll be honest with you: Steve's story was still being written as I wrote this book. But in my experience, a leader in the middle knowing what those problems are and struggling to solve them while implementing the company's plan is far better than a leader having success but not understanding the problems and serving down by protecting up.

You're Doing It Wrong. Yes, You.

Too many leaders in the middle have similar problems to Steve. In fact, the week I spoke to Steve I heard similar complaints from two other clients. For example, Susan had an issue with implementation of a new CRM tool. Despite being a strong manager, she feared making the employees use the tool would make them less successful and they might quit. Did it matter that the company spent hundreds of thousands of dollars on this tool believing it would maximize the success of the employees, the company, and the clients? No. She resisted it and was exploring a new way. She chose to protect her team from the change she feared and defended up instead of serving up.

On the face of it, Susan might seem justified with her defense. This was the second CRM tool the organization had tried to implement in the last two years. The first one had struggled to achieve success and employee buy-in. But that justification only works if the tool was the problem, and the tool wasn't the issue. It almost never is—nor was it her bosses. No, the issue was Susan used it as an excuse for not serving up by demanding down. The issue was her fear of change and demanding that she and her people learn something. The only way to overcome it was to see the tool as valuable not just for the company but as something the team could leverage for the success of the company thus making themselves more valuable.

As we will cover more in depth in Part 7, leaders in the middle mistake resistance as a way to increase their leverage and power when it is the exact opposite. Compliance isn't the path to success either. It's serving up by demanding success not making excuses, which is what Susan learned when she demanded that her team (and she) master the new CRM tool. She took away any idea of "negotiation" from her followers. She made it clear she wasn't asking for feedback on the company's decision or the need to list all its problems. The CRM tool was not what was being evaluated—they were. She demanded they all use the tool and update it with all the knowledge they had on their customers to be more aware of any issues those customers had and anticipate any future needs. Once the benefits of learning and implementing the CRM tool was viewed as more valuable than the fear and pain of implementing it, they stepped up to the challenge.

Next up was a senior leader from a Fortune 100 company who wanted me to help find a way to deal with Jonathan, one of his directors. Jonathan's issue was a bigger, more evolved version of Steve's. He had been a leader at the company for years but had constantly been passed over for promotion. Everyone liked him, but few liked working with him, even when the team was successful and especially when it wasn't. He was the leader in the middle that his bosses would joke about: "Who gets Jonathan this time?"

What could be done about Jonathan? What was wrong? Could he be saved? Turns out, Jonathan wasn't in need of saving. He was just misguided.

When I spoke to Jonathan, his bosses, and his teams to understand what was going on, I found a similar theme in what they said: Before any project, Jonathan always told his people that he would protect them from his bosses and the organization. When his team missed their goals or failed, he had them write reports on the reasons (most of those reasons were beyond their control). He would then turn those reports into his bosses, explaining that it was not the team's fault; they were "doing everything they could within their control."

Because of this constant blaming of others and the company, Jonathan was difficult for his bosses to manage because he never served up—never served *anyone*. By playing the blame game, Jonathan treated his team members as victims; they often felt helpless and incapable of achieving their goals. At the same time, his bosses knew that no matter their expectations for his team, he would spend as much time finding reasons why his team couldn't meet them than trying to achieve them.

If Jonathan, like Steve and Susan, shifted his mindset from defending up to serving up, he would change how he engaged his team and start coaching them to exceed expectations instead of protecting them from those expectations.

The Serve Up Mindset

As I said at the start of this book, I spent most of my corporate career in middle management as a regional manager of stores and employees, a sales manager of a business-to-business sales team, and a director of sales managing managers. I found success in each of these positions because I lived by a simple principle a mentor once told me: "Your job is to make your boss look good."

These were not just words to me; they became the foundation of my leadership belief system. Sure, I made mistakes, and sometimes I was not sure why my boss asked me to do things. But I didn't let fear or my ego get in the way of serving my boss to make him look good. What serving up really came down to then is the same thing it comes down to in the situations faced by Steve, Susan, and Jonathan, or in most situations: accountability instead of fear of the new, the different, failure, that your people will quit . . .

Stop the fear and shift your mindset! Fear in business is nothing but worry about what might happen. No one and nothing is to blame for that fear consuming you as a leader except *you*—not the tools, employees, or your boss's expectations. Your problems are leadership issues compounded by defending up instead of demanding down.

If the expectations as explained to you are not unethical, illegal, causing you or anyone else physical pain or abuse, or immoral, your job is to serve, not defend, up!

If the expectations are that employees will be more successful, the company will achieve its goal, and clients and customers will win, your job is to demand your people achieve that goal. And if your people fail or decide they are no longer a good fit? So be it!

Be Better, Faster, Stronger

On the old TV series *The Six Million Dollar Man*, Steve Austin—an astronaut left barely alive from an accident—is turned into "The Bionic Man" to make him "better, faster, stronger." My client Steve was more than alive, generating six million dollars in revenue for his company when I started working with him. Like Susan, Jonathan, and many leaders in the middle, he was not unsuccessful. Yet he still needed to be better, faster, and stronger. But he didn't need a bionic arm or legs. He just needed to shift his mindset to serve up instead of defending up.

It all comes down to human nature: We know change and risk are sometimes necessary. Yet in the face of them our instinct is comfort (flight), not change (fight). In this case, that means leaders in the middle defend up, because they not only feel it is the nice and noble thing to do but also because it allows them to keep doing what they're doing. It's uncomfortable to demand more and push harder.

But while defending up might be comfortable short term, it's actually harmful because it maintains the status quo. It doesn't compel you or your people to expect more from yourselves. It encourages complacency. It compels you to justify the team's limitations and your own instead of demanding more. What team wants that?

By changing one's mindset to serve up by demanding down, you become a leader your boss and team respects. Your boss respects you, because you don't demand anything but the best from your people. Your people respect you, because you want them to be better and thus strive to achieve what you empower them to do. And if anyone calls you a suck-up? Well, they just don't get it.

CHAPTER 2

Serving Up Is Not Sucking Up

As he launched into the most important part of his presentation, the regional vice president's microphone started having problems. This was an important presentation from one of the most senior people at my company. There were only three regions, and each had only one VP who answered directly to the C-suite. In the audience was that entire C-suite, as well as the two other regional VPs and every member of their executive teams. And this guy sounded like a wireless call cutting in and out. None of us could understand him.

Thank you . . . the most important . . . if you consider last year's . . . for growth . . .

As a regional director, my boss was one of the other regional VPs, and all I could think at first was *thank the lord it wasn't him presenting.* But before that thought turned into any action on my part to help, the regional director who served the VP on stage jumped up out of his seat, ran to the AV team, and grabbed a new mic so his boss could continue his speech. The whole exchange took only minutes.

While all this was happening, the person next to me nudged my arm and whispered, "Look at that suck-up. His daddy's mic is not working, so he kisses his ass so fast that he gets him a new mic before the AV team does." I didn't respond, but as the mic was being wired up he continued: "Man, if my VP's mic does not work, he can get his own new mic. He's a grown man. I'm not here to wipe his nose."

No, he wasn't. Neither was I. Neither was the regional director whose VP was quickly back on the horse and riding through his presentation. Only one of us, however, saw what the regional director did as sucking up, not serving up. And that wasn't me.

Jealous Much?

Listen, I get it. Perception is reality and there is a fine line between sucking up and serving up. But even if the action is the same, sucking up and serving up could not be more different.

Sucking up, or ass-kissing, is a selfish act of manipulation meant to take advantage or mislead someone. Sucking up is wiping someone's nose—a gesture to make oneself feel needed and recognized by somebody and/or as a means to get something else. Whatever the act, it's never about kindness. There's always a hidden agenda.

Serving up is a selfless act of support for your boss and the vision and direction of the organization, no questions asked. It's about respect, not recognition or feeling wanted, and never about manipulation and hidden agendas.

If you are in a situation where someone calls you a suck-up, ask yourself: Are you genuine or insincere? Are you being gracious and respectful to those you answer to, not from a position of weakness, but from a position of power in serving them to better lead your team and serve the company as a whole? If so, then the people who serve you will have the same respect for you, your bosses, and your company. They will never see you as a suck-up. Suck-ups never serve anyone genuinely and never hesitate to sacrifice those not in a position of power to improve their stature. This makes them not only less likable and less desirable employees but also untrustworthy. If you are serving up, doing what it takes to work hard and respectfully to make you, your boss, your team, or anyone important to your professional and personal life look good, be better, solve problems, and grow, then keep doing it. You will find recognition and reward without asking for it.

Now, does that mean that when you serve up you can't try to align the organization's goals with your own or ask questions about how to do what the company needs you to do? Of course not. It only means that serving up starts from a place of positive intent and not blaming anyone or anything for your problems. Those who call you a suck-up for that are almost always jealous of you and how your career flourishes as you lead with humility and a great desire to achieve. The irony is they would act in the same way if given a second chance! But they would not reap the same rewards even if they did because their motives would be insincere and viewed suspiciously.

In my fifteen years in corporate America, I got promoted for results, not being a yes-man. While I kept moving up in the organization, building bigger and better teams that delivered results and made my bosses look good, those leaders and team members who called me a suck-up left the company, struggled to keep steady jobs, and were often miserable. And boy do those people know how to hold a grudge; some of those people would still call me a suck-up today! *Fifteen years after I left a job* people have told me that so-and-so who got passed over for my promotion heard my name and said the same things about me that I heard back then: "The only reason he got the job is because he sucked up to the bosses."

These people don't get what it means as a leader in the middle to serve up. Those who learn to serve up understand their value but have the ability to live humbly. The others who reject its premise are like that guy next to me at the corporate meeting. Let's call him Mr. Bitterman.

I knew Bitterman's story. He felt for years that he was overlooked for promotions. That he was better and smarter than everyone else. He wasn't, of course, but Bitterman *did* have all the skills and knowledge needed to accomplish great things. He simply lacked the desire and humility to serve up to success. As he was unwilling to do that, anyone who did was automatically a suck-up, like the director who scrambled to get his boss a new mic.

For the two years following that meeting, Bitterman changed bosses several times. Each boss liked what they saw on paper but found him difficult to work with in the end. He complained about others and insisted he deserved more right up to the day he was fired.

As for the regional director who grabbed the new mic? He continued to excel in our company until he took the opportunity to start his own company—with the blessing and help of his VP! He has found success at the top and is now making ten times what he made as a leader in the middle. All because that regional manager understood one basic fact: *You get paid to serve and help those you call boss.*

A Suck-Up Sucks Down Too

We've all been in this position: Your boss gives you a direction or delivers a message about a change that you do not agree with and that will seemingly affect you negatively. You think your boss is ill informed, does not really understand the business, and just might be crazy. This leads to feelings of confusion, anger, fear, distrust, and unhappiness. Or all of the above.

Those are all honest reactions. What happens next depends on your mindset. Those with the wrong mindset usually fall into three categories:

1. **"Defend Up, Protect Down"** leaders have the mindset to reaffirm their need to be correct and complain constantly to the people they serve (like my clients Steve or Susan). They fear taking action and suffer from analysis paralysis. When they do act (*if* they do), it is often tentative and lacks commitment, which translates to similar actions from the team.

Thus, every action a leader with this mindset takes has the potential to undermine their company's and leaders' direction.

2. **"Demand Down Suck-Ups"** are a worse version of the "Defend Up, Protect Down" leaders. They try to be good soldiers, saying things like, "Whether we agree or not does not matter. It is what it is, and we are going to line up." They then tell their boss how awesome everyone thinks the plan is and believes in it 100 percent. Although that might sound like demanding down and buy-in in a military fake-it-until-you-make-it kind of way, these leaders still undermine their bosses and the company direction, because they actually lack belief in the company's decision. They're just doing what they're told. This is *not* a lower-level leader in the middle issue. As one senior manager told me, "I am the senior VP by title, but really I am just a glorified frontline manager, because I just do what I am told."

3. **"Defend Up Suck-Ups"** have the worst mindset of all: They tell their employees that they don't agree with the decisions at the top and that they're wrong. They blame upper management or the company in general for these supposedly bad decisions and side with the employees, painting all of them—including the leader him- or herself—as victims.

Don't play the victim. Serve up. And remember: *Serving up does not mean leading with no questions asked.* When you do things or follow directions you don't agree with or understand and never ask questions to understand, you do what every company fears most: check the box. You are sucking up to the direction, no questions asked. You are being a "yes man" or "yes woman" instead of a "how person" who faces those feelings of confusion, anger, fear, distrust, and unhappiness, resists questioning the direction, and then asks good questions about *how* the company sees things being implemented. This not only shifts your mindset but also your perspective.

Change Your Perspective and Challenge Your Assumptions

It's natural to see things from our own perspectives. In business, perspective gets in our way the same way it does in life. When we consider how change and new directions and decisions will affect us and the people we're accountable for, we react in two different ways: When we think the decisions will have positive consequences, we embrace them. When we think they will have negative consequences, we instinctively retreat to the status quo or do only what feels comfortable to mitigate the negative feelings and "pain" of change.

Consider that from the experience of one of my leader in the middle clients, John. John is a sales engineer for a high-tech company that manufactures technology and equipment for drilling companies. He called me one day to say he was frustrated with his boss and the company. His boss just informed him that they were realigning the team and shifting responsibilities. He felt his boss was making a huge mistake and that she did not truly understand the negative impact this would have on him and his team. Her decision was wrong and no one there truly understood how the business runs from the frontlines. They should have consulted him first.

John concluded by telling me he might have to leave his job. "What do you think, Nathan?"

I think you have worked there for five years, and prior to this decision, you thought your boss was awesome and super smart and the company was better than the competition.

"What does that mean?"

Take a step back and look at this from a better and bigger perspective. If prior to this decision your boss was smart and your company was awesome, then that has not changed. So this latest decision is one made by an awesome company and a smart boss, and maybe you don't see that because this time the decision appears to affect you. The key word is "appears." But all the decisions they have made affected you. They just didn't appear that way. You are basing your decision about the future on how it appears in the present.

John paused for a moment and agreed that he might not be looking at the big picture and how this decision benefits the company and the team as a whole. So he did exactly what we discussed: He gave his boss and the company the benefit of the doubt. He spoke to his boss about the issue to get a better understanding of the decision, not to prove him wrong. He then asked his boss how she would recommend he move forward and learned what he and his team needed to do differently to make them successful.

After a few months, John saw the benefit of the decision. Although he was right that it made his job a little harder at first, he was wrong overall. After those initial inconveniences, he recognized it was the right decision and the team achieved greater success. John is still at that company today and would now tell you the decision was the right one. Things were better in the long run than his perspective at the time allowed him to see.

The questions are: What happens next time when a decision appears to have negative consequences for John and his team? Will he keep his current perspective? Will he protect himself from the pain and flare his ego, or serve up? Most decisions or directions upset leaders in the middle like John not because they feel the actual decision is bad but because no one asked their opinions: *If they cared, they'd ask me! They don't respect me or my team.* In turn, these leaders fail to assume positive intent on the part of leadership, deny that those leaders above them may know more than their own perspectives allow or warrant, and thus refuse to serve up.

As you will see in Part 3 of this book, when it comes to serving up, we must assume that our boss and those who lead us have more information and more visibility to make the best decisions for the company and us. In many cases, we may never know why the decision is made until much later, if at all, even at companies that are very transparent. Although we would all like to be consulted on these changes—or feel like we are important enough to the organization to be asked our opinions—the truth is, most of us are not. We can't let that perspective lead us to believe that our bosses and company do not have a full understanding of the consequences of the decision.

I'm not saying that a leader in the middle can't ask for understanding and still serve up, but you must make that your real intent: seeking to understand and not to judge or criticize. Sure, you have a right to an opinion and many bosses like being challenged—wait, no, they don't. Not unless they ask for feedback and invite you into the process. Yes, all bosses should treat their people with respect and not judge or assume they will resist the changes. But unless those decisions violate your principles or the law or would cause something or someone pain, you need to buy in by serving up.

Your Belief Determines the Action

As a leader in the middle, I didn't always understand the reasons behind some of my company's changes, but I committed myself and my team to go full speed in whatever direction we were told. If it was the wrong direction, we would turn and go full speed in a different direction without fear. The cool thing about this mindset is that it is all about belief, and belief does not require proof. Things that can be proven don't require belief and faith. Big decisions and changes in direction in business by necessity require those things because they are all about speculation.

So when I hear a leader in the middle say, "I would believe it if I knew it was the right decision," it makes no sense to me. *Everything* is about believing without proof or even reasons why. Remember: Your power as a leader in the middle is not determined by whether or not you made the decision but by your belief and commitment to serve your leaders by leading your team to success without ever understanding the "why." Your power and value are based on your mindset, discipline, perspective, and execution, not by who made the decision.

Leaders in the middle must share the company's expectations with their employees and hold them accountable to the belief. If everyone is accountable to the belief, then leaders won't have to worry about holding their people accountable to the activity.

Do you find that a tough pill to swallow? Remember: Leaders in organizations have different levels of visibility to decisions and for one reason or another can't share all the information with their employees. Sometimes the decision being made is based on anticipated changes in the marketplace or industry that the organization wants to get ahead of, but the needs are not as clear today as they will be in the future. I agree that businesses and leaders should always be as forthcoming and transparent as possible, but unless it is something illegal, immoral, or against your values, your paycheck does not come with a requirement for anyone to prove to you why the decisions the company and its leaders make are right. This belief is not based on weakness, rather it is based on the conviction of serving up.

Can't follow that rule as an employee or leader? Don't feel your boss or company has the right intentions or right plan? Quit or transfer to a leader you can believe in. Do the same for the people you lead or let them go. Don't let those unwilling to serve change the mission—even if they suck up to you.

CHAPTER 3

Serving Peers, Coworkers, and Customers

For four years in a row, I had spoken at my client's annual senior leadership meeting—a high-level meeting of managers who manage managers. After my last event with them, we discussed the serving up, across, and out mindset, and they decided to take action on what we discussed the following year: They would have senior leaders of all the different divisions share what they do and then discuss how they could serve one another better.

Serving across to peers and teams in other departments and divisions in order to gather different perspectives and see new opportunities and ways of doing things is an important concept. The intent is not to share what a leader of a department needs from others, but rather discover what that leader's team could do to serve the other departments. It's from a giving position, not a receiving position. If leaders in the middle can find ways to serve out this way, meaning serving the other departments in the organization by giving rather than receiving, they in turn will be served. This principle applies to other parts of our business as well, as we need to serve out to our customers, clients, and external partners.

The challenge, however, is not to do this at one annual meeting but to sustain it all year long. Leaders in the middle need to own this and be empowered from the top down to take the next steps and find ways to keep serving across and out on an ongoing basis. When the leaders in the middle lead with this serving mindset and accompanying actions, the people who follow this leader will do the same. Those they serve will see them making the entire organization better, not just their team.

My client did this and several months later was seeing greater success than ever before. The CEO told me that since our serving up, across, and out sessions they continued to drive the mindset through the organization and demand it of their leaders in the middle. The leaders in the middle owned the direction and the result has been a cultural sea change with silos being removed and leaders and departments trying to "out-serve each other." He calls it a "culture you can see and feel." And you can have it too.

Serving Those Beside Us

During our executive coaching sessions, Ken talked with me about his frustration with the design and creative team at his company—the "team in the back." Ken is a leader in the middle on the sales team, responsible for ensuring the sales team hits its quotas and sells the best product for the client. He recently had a meeting with his boss and the manager of the design team. During the meeting, they discussed several customer orders that were delayed or wrong. Ken said the manager of design blamed his sales reps for not completing the paperwork and when they did it was inaccurate. Ken responded that the designers weren't doing what the customer wanted and wouldn't attempt anything outside their standard operating procedures. He also said the design team did not care about the customer's project and looked for any reason not to do the job, rather than finding any way to get it done.

I asked Ken to consider all these things in our coaching session. *Is the manager correct? Do the sales reps not complete the paperwork, and is it incorrectly done sometimes?*

"Yes, but it's not their fault. The customer makes changes, or they are so busy they forget things."

Then that is not what you need to focus on. It's how to do it.

My direction to Ken was if each leader focuses on getting their own houses in order instead of worrying about the other leader's team, we start making improvements. Clean your side of the street and then you can serve across and help others clean theirs. *What would happen if you asked the design manager what you and your team could do better to help the designers be happy and more successful?*

"The design team would love that, though some of their needs may not be doable."

Don't you think just you asking and seeing what could be done would start to bring the two departments together?

Ken agreed it might and that it was worth a shot. He called me a week later and said things were much better between him and the design manager. When I asked him what changed, he said the morning after we spoke he went to the design manager's office and asked to see the mistakes his team was making so he could make sure they improved their work. That lead to them discussing other issues, most of them small in scope, but still major issues to his team.

Ken told me one of the best things that came from the meeting was that on his way out, the design manager told Ken that if there was something special he needed to just let him know and he and his team would find a way to make it happen. For the first time in months he felt the two leaders were truly working together. The words I had for Ken besides "congratulations" was to make sure he kept his word and served the design team by holding himself and his team accountable to serving out every day.

How often have you heard similar stories and complaints that started Ken's story from people you know and work with? "It's their fault, not ours." Or, "It's that department's responsibility, not mine." Or, "That person is in charge, not me." Or, "Why the heck should I care or understand what that department is doing?" And that's just some of the things you hear out loud. The things you *don't* hear are from the haters. The ones who have been conditioned to think that anyone who is not working for you is working against you. That others are threats to your leadership position. That serving others besides those above you is a sign of weakness. That anything that can't help you get ahead is a waste of your time.

Annoying but not surprising given the size of the silos that divide people, teams, and departments in many businesses.

Too many leaders, departments, and teams are selfish and siloed. They view collaboration and cooperation as a path to ruin or, at the very least, sharing the reward and recognition. Asking for help? That's weak. Working together? That just means you can't do it yourself or admitting you're wrong, right? To these leaders in the middle, serving peers is always negative.

Well, haters gonna hate, and they are definitely gonna hate what I'm about to say: Ignore them and break down the silos to connect with those who feel otherwise. Every organization has its "us versus them" battles from these silos. Operations blames sales. ("They don't sell it right.") Marketing digs in against engineering. ("They designed and manufactured it wrong.") My favorite is finance battles *everyone*. I loved my finance team, but they never saw anyone as anything but an adversary.

It Does Not Have to Be This Way

Serving across the company doesn't need to wait for a major change or major achievement to happen. It's about changing the mindset and belief through regular decisions and actions to serve. That way when a problem does occur, there is already an intent to serve across. I learned early in my career that breaking down these silos and serving these departments—transparently and genuinely before any issues arose—made me and everyone around me more successful in our jobs.

When I sold pagers, I would ask the inventory department what inventory they needed moved and focus on those products. In turn, if I ever needed some special help on a sale, the inventory manager was always willing and able to help. Then, five years later as a regional director, I even tried to break bread with finance! I had the head of the regional finance team share their financial goals, we shared ours, and together we committed to serve each other. Our work helped our president achieve the top performance award at the company, and although our efforts were only a small part of the overall success, they led to more sharing and serving across the company. For example, one of his finance managers met with one of my managers to help create a report that compared revenue and expenses by retailer for the entire nation. This was not a mandate from his boss, rather it was something my manager mentioned we could use to support our field employees. The finance manager got to work and delivered us the exact tool we needed. He did it without our even asking. He was just serving across as our partner on one winning team.

But the moment I fully understood the real power in serving across and knew everything I had been taught about the "right" way to do business was wrong was when one of the greatest leaders in the middle I ever worked with asked me to form a partnership. Not in a new company but *within the company where we worked side-by-side for a couple of years.*

Patrick was the director of retail, and I was the director of indirect distribution. In the past, these two divisions were known for their conflicts and struggles with each other. Patrick's team was in charge of making sales in the company-owned stores; my team was in charge of adding retailers to sell more products. It was good for the organization to have multiple locations and different channels for cost and span of control, but before Patrick took over his team, our teams it viewed as competition, resulting in less income for the teams and more customer service problems. After Patrick started, however, he and I met, and we changed all that. I shared with him what I had shared with the previous director (and had fallen on deaf ears): My team's intent was to serve our peer departments. He jumped up and said, "I could not agree more. It's up to you and me to show our teams how to serve each other." Patrick meant it. He told me we would make it clear to our 600-plus employees that we are on the same team and our goal will be to support each other.

The result was not just our success but the breaking down of silos across the company in our California market as the change was felt immediately and rippled throughout the organization. Now, when an indirect retailer needed help, the retail store was the first to offer help. For the first time, it did not matter where a customer purchased a phone. It just mattered that they were a customer. The following year, the indirect team opened up more than fifty third-party locations and every location was approved by the retail team before moving forward as Patrick considered not only how it would affect his stores' sales but also with a concern for the retailers' success.

Before it had been rare that the sales channels lacked conflict; now they not only worked together, serving each other and helping one another succeed, but also became friends. Soon the California market, previously one of the worst performing markets in the country, became one of the best as our "serve out" mindset even affected our customers who believed we cared about them because we cared about each other.

Three Steps to Break Down Silos by Serving Across

1. Share with your people the serve across mindset. Let them know this mindset will be mandatory and is a key principle of the team. Show them why it is important to serve out and how it will benefit not only the other teams but also your team as well. Then demand this mindset every day and only keep people who demonstrate this mindset. Think of it as "we must" not "we get to."

2. Go to another department, division, or team and share your intent of serving across and your goals for your team and the company with other leaders in the middle. Ask those leaders in the middle to join in a common goal of owning their teams while serving the other teams. Once the other leaders in the middle embrace the mindset and commitment, don't waste any more time. Ask them what your team can do to serve them. Listen with the intent to learn and achieve and not to defend or say, "We already do that." Instead, take note and do it better.

3. Don't just stop with one department or division; work your way around the entire organization and mandate that your team do the same thing. That's the only way to break down these silos that have existed for generations—silos not built by malicious behavior but just a lack of communication and understanding of how to reach out using a serve across mindset.

Simply put, serving others (your peers and coworkers) across the company, only makes you a better leader in the middle and creates a winning workplace.

It also helps you, your team, and your company win the marketplace. That's because serving across your company opens you up to new perspectives that help serve our teams and customers better.

Serving Outward

How often do you hear about companies saying the key to success is customer service, yet it's one of their greatest struggles? Many leaders in the middle experience bad customer service every day in other businesses but when asked about their own departments will say, "My company offers great customer service." Let me tell you this: Nine times out of ten when I hear a leader in the middle say that, they sound like a parent bragging about how their kid is going to be a professional athlete. That's likely not true, just like it's not true that your customer service team is serving better than everyone else.

Like serving up and across, the solution requires a shift in mindset to change the culture of what it means to serve out to our customers: The key to great customer service is to become great customer servants. This is more than a semantic change; it's a change in mindset that requires discipline and execution.

Your people must have the mindset of wanting to be servants to their customer.

Mindset

Think back to the question of how you would treat an important guest who came to visit your home. Say you had to serve that person a meal. Would you offer the best of what you have or microwave the leftover Chinese takeout from Tuesday? I would hope the best of what you have.

Now, what if that person were important but really, really mean? You don't like this person, but you can't avoid him or her. What do you serve? The same thing! We serve to be rewarded with a paycheck, appreciation, and most importantly, a sense of significance regardless of how the customer responds. Let's not let the reactions of others determine our servant actions. You never know: You could be the one who helps those people overcome whatever pain or frustrations they may be having.

A servant's mindset says, "ABS" (Always be serving):

 ▷ I want you to feel special.
 ▷ I want you to feel appreciated.
 ▷ I want you to feel important.

▷   I want you to feel cared for.

▷   I get to serve you.

▷   Doing all this isn't just my job, it's my purpose!

Challenge yourself and your team to execute serving out by finding ways to do servant activities. What would shock our customers (in a good way)? What one change would they most appreciate? This doesn't require more money, just more effort at communicating with a customer servant mindset. Show your customers you care with more urgency.

The hard truth is that most customers never see the work we do for them; that goes for everyone from salespeople to doctors, engineers, farmers, and bankers. Customers judge us on how we *serve* them. I have found that when I offer to serve the unhappy customers, they become less unhappy.

As servants our mindset needs to be: No matter how good we are at customer service, we can do even better. We must strive to be better servants, just like professional athletes must always strive to play better, no matter how many awards or championships they have. In other words, serving customers requires a mindset that is a choice. If you don't like that choice, get out of the service business. If you do, you need to have the discipline to sustain that mindset through the good times and especially the bad. This discipline starts with the leaders in the middle who must remain committed when they are tired, frustrated, hurt, or just in a funk because it is their purpose to make a positive difference to the customer. They must be so committed that they will not let the uncommitted distract them or get in their way.

The most powerful aspect of your mindset it not to allow others to take your purpose away from you—or stop you from acting. This applies to everyone we serve out, across, and up to! It does *not*, however, apply when serving the people who work for us. I did not forget our employees; I left them out on purpose, because to serve our employees is to coach them, making them better, showing *them* how to serve up, across, and out.

That's the next step.

CHAPTER 4

Start Serving Up Now!

Taking the following steps may be a little harder than "Just Do It," but it is easier than looking for a new job and a lot more productive than playing the blame game.

Consider my principle: "My goal is to serve my boss and make them look great!" Then take the time to rewrite it in your own words. Now, write down the actions that you will need to serve that principle. Here's a sample list to get you started:

- ▷ Give my bosses a daily/weekly dashboard report so they know 100 percent of what the team is doing.
- ▷ Call them and let them know of any issues or wins for their benefit, not mine.

▷   When given directions, embrace and follow them, giving candid feedback or thoughts when requested or needed.

▷   When I disagree with the direction, assume my bosses have more visibility and knowledge about larger issues or solutions. Ask questions to seek understanding and not to prove one wrong.

▷   Never talk badly about the boss/company to the team, peers, clients, partners, or customers, or anyone else for that matter.

Finally, after you make your list, write down what you desire to achieve from each action. This is key, because many leaders in the middle know what to do but don't do it. The number one reason? The desired result is not worth the work or sacrifice. So know your desired result because it will become the reason you stick with a principle or discipline when the newness and fun of truly serving up has worn off. And when it does, *remember the following actions and achievements gained when serving up.*

Actions

▷   Stop defending up and protecting down. Demand down and serve up.

▷   Know the difference between sucking up and serving up.

▷   Assume positive intent: Your leader and the company have more knowledge about the issues and solutions, and therefore, your perspective may be limited. You can disagree with the direction but still own the decision.

▷ Take direction and ownership, giving candid feedback or thoughts only when your leader requests it.

▷ Ask questions to seek understanding and how to proceed, not to prove one wrong.

▷ Remove complacency and entitlement behavior and remember: Belief does not require proof.

▷ Reach out to serve those peers in your organization.

▷ Servant service beats customer service any day.

▷ Serving creates sales.

Achievements

▷ Positive relationship with the boss, customers, and peers.

▷ Respect and recognition for a job well done.

▷ Growth in career and individual goals.

▷ Being served by your own team of grateful employees.

▷ Shared goals and culture.

▷ Constant positive belief system.

▷ Being a better "you."

The power in effectively serving up (and across and out) is to make these servant actions part of the everyday culture at your company. The key is to share and teach as a guiding principle before the need to ever address a problem, so when there is an issue, the mindset, perspective, and belief is already in place. When the principles are understood and internalized, the execution is constant regardless of circumstance.

PART 2

Coaching Down

The power of coaching down is expecting and accepting nothing less than the best effort and results from yourself and those you lead. Too often, leaders in the middle don't. They refuse to hold people accountable and make excuses for their performance, leaving their teams unable to come up with, let alone implement, any solutions with confidence. That's not serving anyone well, and it's certainly not the path to a culture of accountability that innovates and achieves powerful results. That's like being the work equivalent of those helicopter parents who try and remove all of life's challenges and give their kids trophies for participation.

Coaching down is not about removing obstacles. It's about making your people bigger than the obstacles and empowering them to implement solutions to overcome them.

Why do we try and remove all the obstacles that challenge our people?

Why don't we hold our people accountable to the same things we hold our kids to?

Why do we demand better from and punish the people we love most in the world for bad behavior, poor grades, and acting entitled and sullen, but enable that from the people we lead?

Because we lack the "coach down" mindset.

CHAPTER 5

Coaching (Not Managing) Your Team

How many of you wished your employees cared about the business and its success as much as you do?

In my workshops, I often ask leaders this question, and inevitably, every leader smiles and all hands go up.

Okay, that would be a miracle, and this isn't a fairy tale. But everyone with your hands up, what are you doing to try and make that happen?

Silence.

How many of you spend at least one hour a week developing your employees—not telling them what to do but coaching them to help them do it better? Getting together in groups and practicing or scrimmaging and role playing? If you do any or all of these things keep your hands up.

Few if any hands stay up. Would yours? Why not? Your answers probably sound like those leaders in my audiences who tell me their reasons why not.

"It's not because I don't want to do it, Nathan," they tell me, "but what leader has the time to develop employees, teach them, or practice with them?"

Can you see the disconnect between wanting your people to care as much as you do but not having enough time to show that you care by actually spending time with them? The best leaders in the middle know that when they start caring about their employees' professional and personal development, those employees will care more about the business and its success. But that requires spending time with them to make them better.

"I'm not holding my people's hands, Nathan," they tell me.

Coaching down is not hand-holding. It's not about removing obstacles for employees; it's about making employees bigger than the obstacles and not accepting anything less than the desired effort and results. It's about creating a culture of engagement in which people push forward with solutions, not problems.

"Let them fail. Right, Nathan?" they tell me.

True, people who experience failure are far more likely to succeed. But failing (or failing forward, as is vogue to say these days) and setting your team up for failure are two *very* different things. I'm all for accepting failure but not because my team wasn't prepared to succeed. How are you empowering your team to succeed by ignoring them? The number one responsibility of leaders in the middle to their direct reports is to make them better and more successful. That means coaching them.

"I'm not into that froofy crap, Nathan," they say.

[Incredulous stare. Forehead slap.] Coaching down is *not* froofy. (Is that even a word?) It's not about planning fun activities and bonding experiences. It's not about telling your people that everything will be okay. It's also not about letting your people run around like entitled children with bad attitudes or bad beliefs regardless of their success or tenure. It *is* about allowing people to be who they are and supporting their purpose-driven lives but not at the expense of the company. Coaching down comes with real demands.

Coaching Employees to Excellence Versus Managing to Mediocrity

I have written entire books on coaching employees (*The Leadership Playbook* and *The Sales Leaders Playbook*), so consider this section a refresher for those of you who have read those books and a primer for those new to my principles or coaching in general.

Today, it is common to hear leaders in the middle and organizations use the word "coaching" to describe how they serve their employees. And they're right: To serve the people who follow you is to coach them. I just find that most organizations and leaders in the middle like using the word "coaching" and are less interested in understanding what it means, let alone executing a coaching culture. They may want to do it or even feel they already coach. But because most organizations have never taught leaders how to be coaches, they don't actually coach people; they manage them, just like their predecessors did for generations.

In fact, many leaders in the middle think they're coaching when they aren't. The most common example of this is when they and their organizations confuse coaching with feedback. Feedback is part of coaching, but just a part, like post-mortem questions about how it went and what could have been done differently. Those people share their thoughts, good and bad, and give recommended adjustments, if any. That's neither a complete coaching program nor is it even a complete feedback program. It's only feedback after the fact and basically useless if no work and feedback happened *before* the meeting. Essentially, the feedback is about the next opportunity (whenever that is) and is usually forgotten without coaching. In other words, the "game" was over. Feedback becomes nothing more than managing a post-game wrap-up and goes nowhere.

Unless there is preparation and more opportunity for feedback after the fact, this managing rarely leads to better preparation next time. Coaching prepares the people you lead to be successful before any feedback happens, and whether they failed or succeeded in the situation being discussed, the work afterward continues for days, weeks, and months. The feedback from the previous meeting or opportunity becomes part of the coaching and preparation for the next opportunity. The key is to understand the feedback session and preparation are two different events.

Let's break it down: A manager watches an employee engage with a customer in a retail store. After the customer leaves, the manager comes to the employee and asks her how it went, what did she do right, and what would she do differently next time? They discuss the answer. They part ways. But what if that manager were a coach serving her employee? What if she walked up to that same employee the next morning and asked the employee to practice the situation from the day before, so when it happens today, she would be even more prepared? What if the coach and the employee then conducted two or three "scrimmages" of the situation to understand what might happen?

That's what the best professional coaches do for their teams. Why not yours? *Why don't we do it?*

Because of all the excuses I laid out at the start of this chapter and one I did not: We lead from what we have learned, and old habits are hard to break. Why do you think it is so hard to change your eating habits to lose some weight? It's much easier to just keep eating those French fries and buy bigger jeans. But when life and death are on the line and the doctor tells you to stop . . . well, even then it is hard for many of us. We'd rather test the limits of what we like to do (and are conditioned to do)—and French fries are really tasty.

Of course, most days in business are not life-and-death situations, but if you're business is not growing, then it's dying. Even if it is not losing money (yet), it's just dying a slower death by being managed to mediocrity. Managing is the French fries of business—easy to do, mindless, and satisfying as it is happening—but the result over time is dangerous. Managing eventually clogs an organization's arteries and prevents the body of the organization from being the healthiest and best it can be and achieving excellence (that is, innovation and strong growth).

So why do we keep doing it? You ever try to stop eating a tasty plate of French fries (or whatever your Achilles' heel food is)? It's really hard. Those fries are the ultimate comfort food. How can you resist them? Who can show you how? A coach can. She can show you the power of another direction by coaching you.

Note that word: "how." You heard it before when I laid out the principles of serving down and you will hear it throughout this book. "What" you do specifically when you coach is less my concern than how you approach coaching. And like serving down, the how starts with shifting your mindset and challenging what you currently believe as normal in terms of leading your people.

Leaders in the middle need to demand "coaching" from those they serve and "serve" those they lead by coaching them.

The Coach's Intent

I want you to be the best version of you that you can be! Even if you are good, I want you to be great. And if you are great, I want you to get even better. I will not accept anything less because our people deserve a coach that will push them to be their best and nothing less. There is no finish line in employee development. As a leader in the middle, you are never done learning and improving, and thus, you are never done coaching. As long as someone is paying you, you are never done.

Ask yourself this: Who should help your employees be the best at their jobs? You! That mindset is the first step to coaching down successfully: making sure the team is meeting your expectations and is in the best position to achieve success. A coach's intent is not to hire good people and let them do their jobs, rather a coach's intent is to hire great people and make them better. In that way, a coach's job in business is similar to a coach in sports: Make the "players" better; prepare them the best you can for their next opportunity, meeting, or sales call; and then demand they execute.

And that requires you first and foremost to do more.

Coaching down is not passive "hands-off" behavior ("Do your job, and I will get out of your way and support you"). But it's not micromanaging either. It just requires more connection with your team practicing their skills, scrimmaging, and preparing for upcoming meetings or activities so they can own the work and serve you as their boss and the company as a whole.

You must challenge yourself to do more, be better, practice your skills, and demand you have a positive attitude and powerful belief system. It's a bit of a dance, I admit. On the one hand, leaders in the middle want to show the people they lead that they trust them and know they're capable of doing their jobs. But too much "hands off" leaves employees without any ability to learn and grow from their bosses. The leader only gets involved when something goes wrong. That makes coaching impossible. On the other hand, "handsy" micromanagers never learn to trust their teams. They never let their employees learn and grow their own abilities.

How to balance this goes back to intent, which should be clearly stated to your people. For example, this is what I used to say to the people I led: *My intent is to make you better and show how your abilities align with your expectations and behaviors. As a coach, I'm going to give you clear and precise expectations that are not designed to limit your creative ability but rather to become the framework for it. I will expect you to achieve or exceed my expectations on a daily, weekly, and monthly basis. I will spend time helping you develop the skills to do that, because I know what it will take for you and the team to achieve success. I never want you to feel that you must hide from me. We're a team, and I want you to be able to tell me if you need to take care of a family matter or need to do something outside your normal activities because I respect you, not because I want to punish you.*

I really did say that because early in my career I was the person who knew I couldn't tell certain bosses that I was out doing something personal instead of my activity for the day. When the boss would call, and I was on the golf course with my peers to give myself a well day, I would say, "Hey boss, I am just out calling on customers" and make up some report to reflect my activities. I knew I couldn't trust that boss to understand. A few years later, I had a boss who was the opposite: He never cared what I did as long as I did my job. But I quickly learned that was no good either. I wasn't lying, but I also realized I wasn't getting any better at my job.

In fact, I was becoming bored and complacent.

Then, I got a boss who balanced both sides. I loved his candid and genuine style. He told me that he expected me to do my best every day, and the only way he could help me was if he were part of my success. He told me up front to tell him if I wanted to ditch part of a day or take care of personal business, not cover it up. That way, if he needed to find someone else to do a job, he could do it. He then told me that I needed to be willing to do the same for him and the team if they needed me to do more, stay late, or sacrifice. "Our goal is to win, Nathan. If you don't have the same goal or don't want to do more and do better, then you need to find a new team or job."

I didn't, and that was how I started to learn the power of coaching down. And I didn't just survive. I thrived.

CHAPTER 6

Surviving Versus Thriving

My wife likes to garden, and one thing she has learned after killing many plants and vegetables is that no matter how good or healthy the seeds are, if you plant them in bad soil, then they will not grow or produce.

The same is true for our employees. Leaders in the middle who coach down create a soil (a culture) that their people don't just survive in, they thrive and produce great results in. This culture must be informed by team unity, positive attitudes, and a willingness to do anything to be your best every day. You must demand this! But you don't need to be a hard-ass to get those results as a coach.

Joe Maddon, the baseball manager who broke the longest curse in baseball by leading the Chicago Cubs to their first World Series title in 108 years, is obviously a hero to Cubs fans. But even though I'm not a big baseball fan, he quickly became a coaching hero of mine. Not because he led his team to the top for the first time in a century. Not because he challenged his players and pushed them to be the best or that he never stopped (and thus never let his players stop) believing they could win the championship. All great coaches in all sports do that.

The one thing that stood out to me about Maddon was how he got his players to relax the day before a game. After several intense days of practice, he would have thematic dress-up days. For example, one time the players dressed in pajamas to travel to a road game. This serious-fun coaching style created a culture authentic to Maddon and his leadership style and thus fostered a genuine camaraderie among everyone on the team—and reminded them not take themselves so seriously. It's only baseball. No one is going to die.

Therein lies the lesson: Have dress-up days at your office! Okay, most of my clients just texted me to see if I need to see a doctor. I don't. Nor do I think you need to dress up if you don't want to. You just need to create a coaching culture that is healthy, authentic to you, and fun . . . but still focused.

A leader in the middle does not have to be a drill sergeant to coach down and demand results, though most leaders could learn something from those sergeants and vice versa.

Three Things a Leader in the Middle Can Do to Create a Thriving Culture

1. **Mandate that everybody on the team has a positive and powerful attitude.** I mean everybody, even that one person. You know who I'm talking about; make it happen or

make him gone. You owe it to your team to make sure everyone does his or her job and remove any teammates that have a negative impact on others.

2. **Implement a belief system of "we will."** When companies make big changes, your people focus on what they *will* do. When the competition lands a blow, your people respond with *we will win* next time no matter what. This we-will mindset means they don't worry about why something happens, they focus on how they will do better by maximizing a success or overcoming an obstacle. No victims, just victors.

3. **Implement the "Maddon effect."** Make winning and working focused fun. Can you imagine a culture like that? Everyone having positive attitudes. Naysayers shaped up or shipped off. Nothing is a problem, only an obstacle to overcome. Everyone having fun and laughing yet taking their jobs seriously and working harder than they have ever worked before to serve you! Man, that sounds great, right? And it's not a fantasy either. It's what happens when you coach down. But then, to really thrive, you must also sustain it. Thriving means focusing your coaching on the right people in the right way and then taking the time to keep doing it right.

Spend Time with Those Who Deserve the Attention

In sports, coaches spend the most time with the first-string athletes and the superstars. The other players work hard, learn the system, and do the jobs assigned to them but get less time. They spend most of the game on the bench. This is because the coach's time and attention are rewards for being the best—for success and hard work. Everyone gets the coach's respect, but more than that it must be earned.

In business, leaders in the middle tend to do the opposite: spend time with the people who *need* the attention, leaving their top performers who *deserve* the attention alone to do their thing.

I get the thought. "Why do I need to spend time with my winners? They're winners. They're successful. I can leave them alone and make the weaker people better and stronger. I need to turn them into winners." Sounds good, right? Here's why it's not as good as it sounds, or good at all: Focusing your time on those who are struggling, for one reason or another, makes your involvement a consequence of their failure. Your involvement anywhere on the team is seen as a negative. Your top performers go from wanting your attention to wanting to be left alone!

When leaders spend time with people who deserve their attention, other employees see it and see the leaders' time as something they must strive for. *It pushes them to do better—to work harder and deliver better results.* Please don't take this as permission to *ignore* those who are trying hard and struggling. Leaders in the middle must keep building their benches and find ways to spend time with all employees.

As coaches, they must help those who are not the best find success too, whether that is on their team, somewhere else in the company, or in a new company that better fits a person's attributes and skill sets.

But we can't do any of that unless we spend time with all our people "on the field" by practicing and scrimmaging with them.

Learn to Practice

Practicing is an absolute game-changer in creating thriving cultures. Nothing contributes to increased production, talent, and overall success than learning how to implement a powerful practice program. Whereas athletes practice 90 percent of the time, in business our teams practice less than 1 percent. Why is this a problem? Because the difference between our best employee and our worst employee comes down to skills that get developed in practice: interpersonal skills, leadership skills, and communication skills.

Before we continue, let's make one thing perfectly clear: *I'm not talking about training.* Most companies train employees on systems, products, and even throw in some annual development. That's fine but not the same as practicing.

Training is learning something new.

Practicing is getting better at something we already know.

Practicing is not something you do when the need arises. The need is *always* there, so practicing must be done on a weekly basis with all employees, not just the first-string or those who are struggling. Imagine how often our employees would show up to practice if we did not make them. Most of them already think they are good enough. And they might be good, even great, but they are never good enough to stop practicing. None of us are! In fact, the top employees should be expected to practice and be engaged the most, even mentoring those who are the top recruits to the culture as part of their responsibilities.

Practicing is focused on what are often called "soft skills," the ones that are seriously undervalued in most cultures: serving and engaging customers, asking questions, dealing with upset employees . . . There are countless topics that could be practiced over and over again.

The key is to keep it fun. Anyone who played sports as a kid knows the difference between coaches who made practicing fun and engaging and those who ran it without a smile on their face, as if having fun at practice was the equivalent of laughing at someone clubbing a baby seal. The process of practicing is, by its nature, repetitive and redundant. Yet that's how we learn: by repeating the task and learning to apply it in different situations.

This is the case with anything we do as a leader in the middle to serve up but especially when coaching down. Simply put, it's the leader in the middle's job to mandate that everyone practice. Expectation and accountability—those are the keys. To create a culture that mandates practicing, leaders in the middle should hold weekly practice meetings to motivate and develop the team.

Turn those boring staff meetings into powerful practice meetings. Spend forty-five minutes to an hour (no more):

▷   Teaching a topic or skill (such as handling customer billing issues).

> ▷ Discussing the process and needed steps.

> ▷ Doing what every kid knows is the best part of practice: scrimmage it!

Learn to Scrimmage

This truly is my favorite part of coaching. This isn't about role-playing. That's for the bedroom to spice up a marriage, not a boardroom. Scrimmaging does require getting into character, but it is not about testing employees, which is what traditional corporate role-playing is about: Teach a program and then role-play to prove they had learned it. Forget about that. Scrimmaging is not about testing but preparation to make sure your team executes what they learned in practice before stepping "on the field."

This is why most athletes, kids to professionals, will tell you that they like scrimmaging the most: because it gives them a chance to play without the pressure. They take it seriously but in a relaxed way to test themselves to do their best before game time. What works, they improve. What needs work, they identify. What they want to try before attempting it when the stakes are high, they go for it!

About to do a presentation to a tough client? Don't wing it or go in unprepared, rather teach the skill, discuss the approach, and scrimmage the presentation by bringing in the toughest people you know to critique it. Anything that can be practiced can be scrimmaged. How many times have you left a meeting with a customer, partner, boss, or employee and wished you had handled it differently? Or wish you had seen something coming? If you're like me and you're honest with yourself, most likely more times than you can count.

Next Time, Scrimmage It!

Think of scrimmaging as the communication style of great coaches.

Say you are a leader in the middle and you're getting ready to have a difficult conversation with an employee. How much better do you think you would do in that meeting if you and I scrimmaged that meeting before you really had it? We scrimmage different scenarios, anticipating issues, coming up with solutions in advance, and feeling prepared for what might come and how to help rather than flying blind. As a result, you will be more confident, relaxed, and effective as a leader.

Say you lead a group of inside sales/customer service people. What would happen if every morning you went on the floor and spent fifteen minutes with each person scrimmaging a situation they handled yesterday so that when it happens again today they are better prepared? You can do the same thing with any department—engineering, IT, finance, marketing—because everyone gets better by practicing and scrimmaging as opposed to just doing.

Here's what I predict: Once you embrace the process of scrimmaging, you will find yourself scrimmaging everything. If I talk to four leaders, I will most likely scrimmage in all four conversations. Not because we are practicing, per se, but because we are dealing with a situation that a leader needs to handle, and the best way I can understand the situation is to scrimmage.

And for those leaders in the middle who don't want to scrimmage because they're afraid their employees will find out they are not as good as they thought? Don't worry, their people already think that their boss is not that good, and that's okay. A great coach doesn't have to be a star quarterback to lead a team into action.

Remember: A leader in the middle is humble first. How better to show our humility than scrimmaging and showing our team you can learn and get better too?

That said, scrimmaging is not just for the leader in the middle of front-line employees. In fact, some of the best scrimmages I have done have been with vice presidents and other very senior people helping their leaders in the middle who serve them deal with their employees. As long as you are somewhere in the middle, you need to be the best coach you can be to hold your people to the highest standards.

CHAPTER 7

Hold Your People to Higher Standards

Lynne is a regional vice president for a large tech company. She is a very strong leader and has been promoted several times. As I was writing this book, Lynne and I were discussing the content for a coaching workshop I was doing for her team about leaders and employee expectations.

"Nathan, let me tell you what is scary," she said. "Most of our current employees would not meet the expectations we discuss with our applicants during the interview process."

What do you mean?

"The expectations we are telling applicants they have to meet or exceed during our interviews are *not* the same expectations we have for many of the people who are working for us now. It's scary to think that those we pay currently and who have been with us the longest, we expect the least out of. In some cases, we're accepting less than we would from those we're *not* going to hire."

Whoa. Why do you think you allowed this scary situation to happen?

"It's easy," Lynne said. "As leaders, if we start really holding our people accountable to these expectations, they might quit, and that means less people to do the work, and we have to take the time to hire and train somebody new. It's just easier and less time consuming to accept less."

Double whoa.

Great coaches know expecting less is a recipe for mediocrity and failure. Yet so many companies still do it. Why? Because we have been managing people, not coaching them. *Most of the time, we haven't demanded much of anything of our people.*

Practicing and scrimmaging deals with some of that. But addressing the problem Lynne brings up is to elevate our expectations of our people through coaching down. That means actually taking more time to develop and prepare our teams. As leaders of leaders, we should expect that our followers coach and develop their followers as we leaders must coach them. Managing focuses on correcting people and their behaviors *after* the fact. Coaching is about developing people's skills and behaviors *before* the fact with an intent to prepare them.

What did you say? You want to coach your people but you just don't have the time? Something suddenly comes up? We'll go deeper into time management later in the book, but for now realize that coaching down is about doing what is important and not just what is urgent. The only way coaching down works is if it becomes the core of your priorities as a leader in the middle.

One-on-Ones

A one-on-one is a regular weekly meeting between a manager and a direct report. The intent is to cover three key areas: review weekly activity, prepare for the following week, deal with any accountability issues, and do some personal development with the employee.

These meetings are where leaders can give the feedback and gain insight to help their people be more successful, and even do more scrimmaging on certain topics and situations. The key is: This is a *planned* meeting. Too many leaders I know say they don't need to have a one-on-one because they talk to their direct reports every day. But most unplanned conversations are about dealing with an urgent issue in that moment. How often are they about preparation or scrimmaging or personal development?

The power of coaching through a one-on-one is that nothing is urgent. The only thing that's important is making you and your people better and more successful. The meetings create long-term learning and better prepare for those urgent issues. Most importantly, great employees love the intimacy of one-on-ones. It not only lets them know you care but also makes them feel like leaders themselves.

Floor Days

My cousin Lawrence Shipley is one of the most humble and generous men I have ever met. You would not know that he is the successful owner of one of the greatest donut franchises in the United States with more than 250 Shipley Donuts locations across the southeast.

Some time back, Lawrence and I were talking about business while at his ranch, and he shared with me some problems he was dealing with at his factory. I asked him when was the last time he walked the factory floor. He admitted not for a while. So I shared with Lawrence the walk-around activity I have my leaders do on a regular if not a daily basis: *Every morning, grab a cup of coffee and walk around your factory floor and just say hello to everybody and talk to them. The more they see you, the more they will feel a part of something bigger than a job. You're a good man. Let's make sure those who work for you get to see it.*

Lawrence immediately started doing this and, not only was the problem solved, but also his production increased, morale improved, and he became a better leader for it.

What makes this story great is not just that Lawrence is humble enough to let me tell it to you but that he was already unbelievably successful. Lawrence did not have to do anything. He could have sat in his office and delegated the problem, but because of who he is—grateful, humble, and believing in his purpose and his people—he made sure he demanded more of himself to stay connected.

Do what Lawrence did: Get out of your office and coach from the floor.

   ▷   If you have outside sales people or managers, get out there with them.

   ▷   If you have a factory, put on those safety goggles and walk the floor.

> ▷ If your people ride in cars, get in the cars with them.
> ▷ If your team spends its days in offices, knock on their doors.
> ▷ Demand the same thing from the people you serve!

This is one of the few times you will hear me say leaders deserve anything. They not only deserve this but must demand it. I say "demand" because many people struggle with coaching higher-level leaders. They assume they already know what needs to be done and may be beyond coaching. But what I said before applies to everyone: No one, and I really mean *no one*, is above or beyond coaching. Everyone benefits from practicing and scrimmaging. Everyone benefits from the right attention.

How do you demand to be coached? With genuine intent. Tell your boss that you intend to coach your employees, but to serve up, you need to be the best leader in the middle you can be, and that requires coaching from the people you serve.

If your boss is worth the title on his or her business card, that person will be excited to hear your desire to be coached, welcome your bold statement of humility, and encourage your desire for growth. You may need to design your own coaching program if one doesn't exist or the boss isn't willing, but they are pretty easy to create. All you do is duplicate the coaching program you're doing with your team with you as the one being coached! Then ask to schedule weekly one-on-ones for practicing and scrimmaging in addition to the other agenda points. If all else fails, and your boss truly won't participate, then ask a mentor to take your boss's place; there are no excuses for not doing this.

Remember: Great coaches are coachable. Open yourself up to the possibilities!

CHAPTER 8

Start Coaching Down Now!

All great leaders are not great coaches, but all great coaches are great leaders. This is true because coaching is more about what you do with your employees and being a great leader is more about who you are. Coaching down is one of the most selfless acts leaders can do for their people. It takes time and work, a great deal of discipline and conflict, but most importantly, it takes a leader in the middle to see the value of being coached so they are willing to do the work and make time for it.

To start, do the following exercise, which is similar to the one at the end of Part 1: Serving Down. Consider my principle: "Embrace coaching down as a priority!" Then, take the time to rewrite it in your own words. Now, write down the actions that you will need to serve that principle. Here's a sample list to get you started:

▷ One-on-one meetings.

▷ Floor days.

▷ Practice meetings.

▷ Create cultural "laws" that ensure a successful team (believe in them and expect others
to as well).

▷ Create and give expectations and hold
every team member accountable.

Finally, after you make your list, write down what you
desire to achieve from each action. This is key, because
many leaders in the middle know what to do but don't do
it. The number one reason? The desired result is not worth
the work or sacrifice. So know your desired result, because
it will become the reason you stick with a principle or discipline when the newness and fun of serving down by coaching has worn off. And when it does, *remember the following
actions and achievements gained when coaching down.*

Actions

▷ Embrace that coaching is a number one
priority; you *can't* fit it into your schedule. It
must be the core of any leader in the middle's
schedule.

▷ Commit to your coaching activities—one-
on-ones, ride days, practice meetings—
make them important. Don't let less important but urgent stuff become excuses for not
doing them.

▷ Lay out cultural laws that ensure a successful team. Believe in them and expect others to as well.

▷ Provide expectations and hold every team member accountable to them.

▷ Allow people to be themselves, but have zero tolerance for bad attitudes, gossip, or excuses.

▷ Write down what you desire to achieve from all of the above; know your desired result!

Achievements

▷ Motivated employees.

▷ Positive work environment.

▷ High-quality new hires.

▷ The best results in the company.

▷ Promotion to your next career step.

▷ Keeping your word by keeping your commitment to coach!

PART 3

Serving and Coaching in Uncertain Times

The only thing certain is that things are always uncertain. A generation ago, it would take years for marketplaces to change, technologies to evolve, and competitors to emerge. Today? It can be months. All the principles leaders in the middle have heard about change—adapt or die, know what you don't know, connect to customers in the marketplace—and all of them are true but impossible to achieve if your organization and its culture lack the right mindset to deal with change.

A serve up/coach down mindset sets the tone for, affirms the trust in, and solidifies engagement with our actions in the workplace—even in the most uncertain times.

CHAPTER 9

Changing the Speed of Change

Change management. Leading through change. Change in [fill in the blank].

Whatever you want to call it, change has been an issue in business since the beginning of, well, business. It will always be an issue. Because things change. They just seem to change a lot faster than they did a generation or even a year ago.

I am not just talking about technology. Workplaces and marketplaces are more diverse, and customers are more demanding for everything from value to price to where and how things are made. Competition can come from anywhere in the world to challenge your products and services—and quickly. In any given twelve-month period, most organizations will change their focus or direction several times. Regardless of your industry, the size of your company, where you are located, and who your customers are, most likely every year something will—and *must*—change in the way you do business.

Some changes may be big changes, like a merger and acquisition or a change in leadership. Some changes may be proactive changes in what you sell or the service you provide, such as a technology firm going from selling products or hardware to selling services like cloud storage. Some changes may be reactive changes driven by a need to compete in the marketplace and respond to a competitor that is aggressively taking market share, like a communications company moving to combine services and refocusing everything from sales to engineering to field operations. Some changes may be more everyday, like a change in team or department leadership.

Regardless of your business, the winds of change blow harder than ever, and the only thing certain is that things are uncertain. Right? Yes. But that uncertainty? It has always been there; it's just more prevalent today. And the winds of change? They do blow harder, but they are the same winds that have been blowing since forever. Whatever change you are facing, changing the leadership mindset to one of serving up and coaching down mitigates that uncertainty and allows leaders in the middle to lead at the speed of change today. And not just at the speed of change but *through change*.

As leaders in the middle we must learn *not just to survive and manage through times of uncertainty* but also *learn to lead and grow* so we, our teams, the people we report to, and the organization as a whole can *thrive*, even during times of uncertainty.

This requires levels of certainty and speed that leaders in the middle are uniquely positioned to create.

Forget About the "What" and the "Why." Focus on the "How."

I couldn't possibly understand and cover all the changes facing leaders in the middle even if I wrote a book specific to a department like sales and marketing or engineering or for an industry I have decades of experience in, like insurance or mobile communications. But here's the good news: Specifics of change do not matter when serving up and coaching down.

In fact, leaders in the middle should forget about the "what." What good is experience anyway? Does anything in business look like it did a generation ago? Why then would anyone expect *what* someone did before to translate into experience to deal with change today?

If my kids saw the phones I used when I started working in the mobile phone business (and I always had the latest phone), they'd think it was a child's toy and start laughing. I know this is true because as I wrote this, I showed them one of those phones and they laughed and called me an old man. I grounded them for a week. Okay, a day. Then one of them asked me a question that gave them all a "get out of jail free" card: "Why were phones like that back then?"

I love when my kids ask me why something happened. It shows interest and curiosity . . . to a point. But you know what happens most times after you answer that first "why" question: Dad, why were cell phones like that? Because they were just trying to be phones. *Why?* Because the Internet was something that was only on computers. *Why?* The explaining goes on forever. And ever. I'm tired just thinking about it.

And I realized that's just it. It isn't just the "what" that doesn't matter: It's the endless stream of "whys."

I'm not saying asking is bad, but what is the intent of the "why" question being asked? Too often it is not to listen to understand; it is either to find a hole in your argument, make you prove to them why you are right, or just to ask another question and another without listening. Taking the time to explain "why" often leads nowhere—except to another "why." And another. And another. No answer ever satisfies your kids, and it won't satisfy your people either. *Because "why" doesn't work; we need to stop focusing on the "why" and start focusing on the "how."*

No, Really. Stop! Stop the Why.

It's not that I don't appreciate the curiosity behind a good "why" question or finding your own "why." Simon Sinek's TED Talk and books have tens of millions of people finding their "whys" (i.e., purposes) and the "whys" behind their "whys." I love his concept: Clarity of purpose and making sure you aren't working for bad people or companies that destroy or dismiss its people's purpose is essential. But in day-to-day business, we get so hung up on finding our "why" and asking "why," we never get to the "how."

Think about it: "Why do we manage change?" should not be a question any leader in the middle needs to answer beyond "Because if we don't, we fail."

The real question is what we discussed in serving up: "*How* do we manage change?" The answer to that question has less to do with what experience you have and more to do with the skills and mindset that must be in place *before* the changes happen—before you even get to the "what" of the details and changes. It must be part of the culture and central to the workplace belief system: Your people will follow your lead through change, questioning only to understand direction, *not* challenge it.

Imagine that. What if you just told every employee on your team to "line up or line out!" Don't question the decisions! Just do it, and do it now! That would make this whole "dealing with change issue" go away, wouldn't it? Think about it: There's no need to convince every member in an organization that the change is necessary and should be a good thing. There's no need to focus on the "why" because the "why" is unaffected or unnecessary to know. Buy-in would be immediate and everyone would be focused on the "how," making the organization able to move and change much faster and making change a competitive advantage.

Done! Only problem is that's the military, not business. In business, that approach is a fantasy. Our people would feel insignificant, undervalued, and most likely leave or just do what they were told and no more, collecting a check while they looked to leave. You may be heading into battle when it comes to change in business. You may have even read Sun Tzu's *The Art of War* (or cribbed what you know about it from the movie *Wall Street* like I did). But your people are not a platoon, and no one is going to die (literally) in a corporate fight to stay competitive.

But there is truth in this statement: As leaders and organizations, if we had to spend less time convincing our team members *why* things are changing—eliminating the whole fear of the pain of change and go straight to buy-in—change would be less of an issue. Especially when the best-laid plans go awry and you need a new plan to deal with the change.

The solution for leaders in the middle is somewhere in the middle—between "we need our team members to trust in the leadership's direction" and "the leaders need to value the team members thoughts, insights, and contributions."

Remember: A "How Person" Is Using the Serve Up/Coach Down Mindset

With the serve up/coach down mindset in place, you understand your responsibility to your boss(es) and your people. You understand your job and theirs is not to question why the organization is changing. Instead, you are inspired to focus and act on the how—to be the "how" person: how to successfully implement the change.

As a leader in the middle, your job is to make your boss look good. You must believe that your leader and organization know more about the "what" and "why" than you do when they make decisions about change. You must focus on the "how" when anticipating and facing that change: how to do what you do better and more effectively than anyone else to serve those you report to and the organization as a whole.

As a leader in the middle, your job is to coach the people you lead, and because you have, they already know they are valued. They don't need to worry about the "what" and "why." They just need to prepare for, face, and solve the issues that face the organization, implement the game plan, and not let anyone or anything stop them.

If all that sounds magical and thus a fairytale, understand that's a problem with mindset in general. The status quo by definition resists change. Teams that have been coddled to doubt rather than coached to win are entrenched in that mindset and have the wrong perspective because their leaders in the middle had the wrong perspective too. As a result, they never embraced or understood the power and importance of their positions.

Thus, even before the uncertainty of change set in, there was already an environment of uncertainty. Leaders and their organizations that have a serve up/coach down mindset thrive in cultures of change. Uncertainty is only an *outside* variable that teams must excel in facing. *Within the organization, there is only certainty,* giving it the powerful ability—top to bottom—to move swiftly and embrace any and all change with 100 percent commitment, no matter the situation. *Leaders in the middle control this power by serving up and coaching down.*

Still sound like a fantasy? Let's consider what this mindset allows you to achieve through a scenario from the workplace (a change in leadership) and the marketplace (centralization of services) that should be familiar to most leaders and organizations.

CHAPTER 10

Workplace Change: The New Boss

I had been consulting with a client for a year when I got a call from the CEO telling me that he hired a new vice president to lead his team of frontline managers. This was not a surprise. I knew he had been looking for the right candidate for a while. The majority of my work with this client had been with the outgoing vice president, conducting monthly coaching calls with those same frontline managers on how to coach their employees. I knew she was changing jobs with the organization.

The CEO thought the new VP was a great fit for the team but had a nagging concern that he did not have any industry experience. Based on his last experience with a transition like this, there had been mistrust when the leader had no industry experience. He felt the managers would push back and not show the proper respect. He also worried there would be some resentment from those managers who interviewed but did not get the job. He wanted to make sure the team did not stumble, get distracted, and lose momentum. He knew I was familiar with her team, had a good rapport with them, and wanted my thoughts on how to successfully integrate her replacement.

I told him I did not share his concern. I couldn't promise him a seamless transition with no grumbling or dissent (no one can), but I didn't feel this was going to be a big issue. I explained that the managers had been coached well and served the current VP well. To this point, we had mainly worked with the frontline managers on coaching their teams. But if we extended our coaching to the managers on this change, and they truly understood their responsibility to serve up, the managers would thrive under their new VP just as they had thrived under the previous one.

Still, understanding how to serve up and actually doing it are two different things. Although we spoke about serving up and implemented many of its principles, this would be their first real test of the serve up mindset. To put the CEO's mind at ease, I told the current VP to set up a meeting with the managers to discuss serving up, how they had served her, and what it means to believe in those we follow, not question them. We invited the CEO to listen in and hear the message we gave the team and hear their comments. If they had the right mindset, the managers would already be prepared to believe in the change, adapt to it, and give a new leader the same respect they gave her. They would serve their new boss no differently than her and not question his experience or why he was hired. He would hear that in how they responded.

The Meeting

The meeting started with me reminding the frontline managers how fond they were of their CEO, how they trusted and believed in him. I recalled how many of them had told me how good a man and leader he was. How he would never do anything to hurt the team. This was the same CEO who had decided to bring in a new VP from the outside to lead them. So with this decision, they must believe this is for the best and do everything not just to stay focused and move forward but bump up their energy.

To do this, they had to suspend any doubt or disbelief and assume the new VP will learn the industry and business and use his skills to manage through the changes in the marketplace.

I warned: Don't get stuck focusing on how it used to be. Be the ones that see the benefits of a new way. The old way lasted a long time. Now we must adapt. Be the managers your new boss can count on as that happens—the leaders that own their leadership roles and responsibilities. The new guy is not coming in here to get rid of strong and committed leaders. Play the victim and hurt his success, and thus the organization's, and he will help you succeed elsewhere. Which is exactly what your current boss would do if he were the new hire.

Finally, I addressed the fact that I knew a few of the managers interviewed for the job and that the natural instinct is to be bitter or hurt. My advice was to take that hurt and use it as motivation to learn what they could from the new boss. Believe that he has or knows something you don't. Don't get mad; get better, and ask him to help you. Maybe you'll figure out what gave him the edge. At the very least, when you take that approach, you're showing respect and allowing him to coach you. If you resent him, the only person who will suffer, and ultimately lose, is you.

Let's get excited about the future, focus on how we're going to be better and win, and not on why or why not a decision was made. Great leaders and their teams focus on how to succeed through change while others focus on what and why the things happened.

What happened next? They lived happily ever after (mostly). A year after the new VP took the lead, the company achieved its best results ever and was on pace to exceed that in year two. Did everyone buy in to what I said? No. But that is inevitable. You don't need everyone and can't always expect that. But the top managers who served up had the greatest success, and one was promoted. One manager who refused to serve up left and was last heard complaining at his new company about the boss who cut him loose and playing the victim.

In short, with the serve up mindset and a belief in the leader in the middle, the team never skipped a beat. The managers transferred their belief to the new boss, because they believed in their old boss and the organization. This allowed the new boss to be himself and humble enough to learn the business and industry even while he led his team without worrying about their commitment. A year later, the new the team's year-over-year performance was way up— better than ever before. Most importantly, because the leader did not have to spend time convincing the managers their new VP was good enough to lead and they did not move timidly, they were able to keep the momentum. Not only did the numbers never dip, they started increasing within the first sixty days.

The Belief Created the Culture, and the Culture Created the Behavior

Simply put, as leaders in the middle, most of the frontline managers at the company owned the power they had to serve up and coach down through the workplace change. Too many leaders in the middle don't. Even successful ones do not own the power they have when serving up and coaching down, especially when it comes to leading through change. Instead, they worry. They lose faith in themselves and their teams when those winds of change blow. When leaders in the middle don't operate with a serve up/coach down mindset, they create a culture of doubt, questioning, and fear of upsetting the troops with changes. They will say things like, "The new boss will have to learn their culture and adapt to them, especially as he knows nothing about our company or industry." Forget about the fact that in many cases an organization is bringing in a new leader to change or improve the culture. *They think resistance allows them to keep their power.*

When leaders in the middle have a serve up/coach down mindset and create a culture based on that mindset, their teams are ready for change. They don't see uncertainty or question new leadership, certainly not until that leadership has a chance to succeed. In fact, it is usually the opposite. The leaders have demanded down and the team is energized. They are ready. They expect bigger and better things. They say, "We get what we expect." *They know keeping the power is about being positive with the decision, embracing the possibilities, and believing that the change will bring what they need.*

Athletes embrace this mindset all the time when a great coach or manager leaves a team he has led to great success. If that coach and organization has truly coached the team to win and serve the organization they play for, the team does not just fall apart when that coach leaves and the new one arrives. The players look forward to learning new ideas and approaches that they had not tried before or maybe tried and failed. They appreciate that the new coach brings a different perspective and leadership qualities and are excited by it all. They respond with enthusiasm to the new coach and look to continue their momentum, maximize their performance, and take their game to a higher level. Only those who get stuck questioning the change or stuck in the perspective of the previous leadership get stuck themselves and are either let go or get traded to another team.

Take a lesson from football's New England Patriots, the most successful NFL franchise of the 20th century. Anyone on that team is replaceable, and must be in the long run, because the competition isn't just throwing up its hands and conceding. If the plan changes or a star player gets hurt, you need the team to keep moving forward—even when you are down twenty-eight points in the Super Bowl. The New England Patriots get it: Put too much weight on any one person or piece of the puzzle and the competition will exploit your weakness and win.

In the end, when a change in leadership happens, there are two key perspectives to consider when serving up and coaching down before the change happens:

1. The leaders: The person who hired the new boss and wants to ensure the direct reports embrace him or her.

2. The followers: Employees getting the new boss and facing the change in the workplace.

The Leaders — Coaching Down

Leaders in the middle don't have to soften their approach but don't have to be hard-nosed and bullish either. Approach the team with clear messages and direction without fear.

For example, a leader could say:

Team, I wanted to let you know that your new manager is joining us tomorrow. I feel she is the best fit for our team and helping us get to our next level of success. My ask of you is to give her the same respect you would want if you were the new leader coming in to our organization. Please remember our job is serve our leaders and organization. You can question to understand direction, not challenge it. Remember that everybody is different, and many times, that difference in perspective and behaviors is the very reason why a person may be selected. Differences and challenges are how we grow! I am confident in you as a team and your ability to embrace your new leader's direction. I am grateful for each of you; never stop believing bigger!

The Followers—Serving Up

This does not have to be a negative situation. Rather, it can be a way to challenge those team members to become better and grow, though it is tricky, especially if employees interviewed for the job.

The wrong mindset fueled by poor coaching and an inability to serve up: I can't believe they are hiring this person. He does not know anything about our industry. I bet he will not make it three months. I'll tell you what: He'd better not micromanage us or start making a bunch of changes. We know what works and what doesn't, so he needs to come in and learn how we do things. If he tries to make me do this or that, I will make his life miserable, or better yet, I will quit. I should have this job; the only reason he got the job is [fill in the blank].

The correct mindset fueled by great coaching and an ability to serve up: I wanted that job, but it wasn't to be this time. I understand that this is the direction we are going. So I need to get better at what I do and learn from this. My goal should be to learn the most I can from this new leader and treat him like I would want him to treat me. Ask him to make me better. I want to understand the direction and expectations for the team, so I can be the leader and my team can be the ones they know they can count on to get things done! I understand that it is only a matter of time before I am that new manager taking on a new team, and I want to be able to model the behavior I would want from my new team.

Remember: No one with power and self-confidence gets passed over. Only victims get passed over. Confident leaders understand the other person was a better fit for the job, and next time, they must do better to be the only choice. *They own it.*

Still Think It's a Fantasy?

Many of you reading this may be thinking, "Yeah, Nathan, that would be great, but it's not realistic." My advice is to change your reality and stop creating self-fulfilling prophecies. "Realistic" is what you make it. The way to ensure the correct mindset and eliminate the wrong mindset is to coach the team members on the mindset before the issues arise. Don't leave it to chance. Most leaders want to assume that team members can only believe one way or another. That is true. They only believe one way—your way—if you coach down. If you explain, teach, and live the serve up/coach down mindset, when issues happen, you don't have to persuade, you just have to hold up a mirror to yourself and your team, check your mindsets, and *believe.*

CHAPTER 11

Marketplace Change: Centralizing Services

If you have been a leader in the middle at the same company or part of a team for a growing company, you have most likely experienced the transition from localized services to centralized services. In spite of the familiarity, for most leaders and organizations, this becomes a huge struggle that leaders in the middle and their leaders spend months or even years convincing everyone from the lowest-level employees to the customers and clients that this is a good thing. They conduct hundreds of meetings listening to issues and explaining themselves.

It's hard enough adapting to the marketplace, technology, and the changing needs of customers and leading through uncertain times without spending so much time getting others to let go of the past and believe in the future. I'm not saying there aren't times that bad decisions are made when it comes to services (or products for that matter) or that direction is so poor (as Yogi Berra said, "If you don't know where you're going, you'll end up somewhere else"). I am saying:

The Biggest Hurdles Are Perspective and Ego

Whether leaders in the middle on down understand the "why," the "why" behind the "why," and the "what" is irrelevant. In most situations, the leaders at the top have insights that others don't have. Those leaders must be transparent about what is happening, but they don't need to share everything. Despite what servant leadership says, there are just some things people do not need to know, would not understand, or would get distracted by. Your people must have direction:

▷ They must be given the tools and resources necessary to collaborate, implement the changes, and grow.

▷ They must be allowed to ask questions so the change ends up going where the organization wants it to go, and the answers they get must be honest and complete.

▷ There should be room for feedback from the people who are in the field so leadership at the top stays in touch with what is going on in the market as the changes are implemented.

Leaders should be prepared for extra coaching time through the changes.

But your people do *not* need deeper explanations and meetings upon meetings that sound like a corporate version of Seinfeld's Festivus "Airing of the Grievances." Yet this is what happens when leaders in the middle, and thus the organization, have failed to serve up and coach down—and get stuck on the "what" and "why" instead of the "how."

In the end, most of these meetings are really about the people feeling like they are being listened to and valued, and that the organization cares about their team, customers, and peers. But when you serve up and coach down, that is already in place, and the certainty in the workplace mitigates the uncertainty in the marketplace. The mindset is: The leaders in the middle have compassion and care just as much as we do, only they have more knowledge than us about what is going on. They are willing to listen, follow, and understand. They don't need convincing and trust what we don't see from the top down. This is not because they have been bullied into submission but because the leaders in the middle had fewer egos and more humility to earn that trust and buy in!

Will the centralization (or really *any* marketplace) change what an organization needs to make work? *Who knows and who cares!* Staying the course isn't an option. It never is. If it isn't centralization, there will be something tomorrow that will need to change. The great thing about serving up and coaching down is that the change and uncertainty is *welcomed* because focus stays on moving forward and achieving the "how." If things fail, it won't be because those leaders didn't coach the team to succeed and serve up to make the bosses' decisions look good.

Be Certain with Uncertainty

Let's get back to the situation of centralization of services as an example of what I mean. It's not that the issues specific to centralization—the issue of local knowledge being necessary and lost ("it's different here" and "consistent connection in the community is our service difference")—aren't real and important issues. But leaders in the middle must focus on changing these issues to a positive rather than complaining about the changes. To be certain with uncertainty and certain in our belief in those we follow and serve means we move quicker to resolution without having to debate or be sold on why. The sooner everyone starts heading to the finish line *together*, the sooner everyone can win.

When it comes to centralization or any changes in the marketplace that are service or product based, remember the serve up/coach down mindset and that there are two perspectives: leaders and followers. The leader in the middle is both.

The Followers—Serving Up

The wrong mindset fueled by poor coaching and an inability to serve up: I don't see the point. I don't know why the leader of the company is doing this, and I don't see it, get it, and/or believe it. So I'm right and they're wrong. If not, prove it to me. Prove to me why we should do it because, like I said, I just don't see it. What's the justification? I used to believe in the people and this organization. But now? Now I need to know more, so I'm digging in my heels and questioning everything.

I've said something like this before. *We all have.* Someone who "doesn't see the point" is not a bad person, rather they have the wrong mindset. Our gut reaction is to question, but we need to move past that feeling and trust that the people we have trusted in the past know where we are going and will lead us there.

The correct mindset fueled by good coaching and an ability to serve up: Assume the best. What did Michael Jordan as Coca-Cola's spokesperson say when asked if he liked New Coke (one of the greatest brand failures in beverage history) more than the old recipe? "Coke is Coke. They both taste great." I need to be like that. I must assume if I see the change as a bad decision or even if it is having negative short-term impacts that the benefit is for the long term or for the greater good, not because the past was bad. I owe it to my peers, my bosses, my organization, and the customers that pay us to move forward. I owe it to them to serve them with my belief and all of my effort! I'll suspend my judgment and just make sure I understand the direction to get where we need to go.

What Will You *Do?*

I witnessed the power of the willingness to suspend judgment firsthand when I took over as the director of a sales team that was struggling in a difficult market. We faced some tough decisions about everything from pay to staffing. I had been there for a couple of months and was well into my reorganization when one of the managers came back from maternity leave. She had been promoted in the weeks before she left, and now she returned to a new job only to face a new boss—me. And the rumors about me were terrible. "This guy is going to fire everybody." "He is increasing all our hours." "He has ridiculous expectations and is going to hold everyone accountable to them."

The manager and I had a meeting scheduled for the day after she returned, and we started out with the usual introductions. I asked some questions about her and how the baby was. After the niceties, we got down to business. I let her know the new team of eight full-time employees and 100 temporary salespeople she was taking over was one of the most unprofitable in the market as well as the most expensive. Changes needed to be made immediately, as in the first hours after she left my office. These changes included sending her eight full-time people into the field to train the sales reps, getting rid of those reps below a minimum standard, and cutting their hourly wage basically in half to focus on commission. That way, those who sold the most would make the most money.

All of this was a lot for anyone to process and deal with, but this leader in the middle looked me in the eye, smiled, and said only three words before she left: "Consider it done." Within forty-eight hours, she had met with everyone on the team and rolled out the new organizational structure, overall strategy, and sales plan. Within three months, her department, which had lost tens of thousands of dollars a month, turned profitable as the worst reps left and the strongest ones thrived. Within twelve months, her team was one of the top in the country.

It was all because this leader in the middle owned her responsibility and served up to me and coached down to her team. She did not let the changes or the fear of the unknown startle her or get in her way. Instead, she used it as power to challenge herself and drive her forward. She turned that power in to belief—belief in the company and the leaders who hired me. She did not focus on *why* my decisions were being made; she focused on getting it done and making her team better to achieve our goals.

In other words, this leader in the middle let go of the past and faced an uncertain future with a certainty in what she was doing, knowing the organization had her back. She didn't romanticize the past. She looked to the future. Ask yourself: Who *never* gets driven crazy by changes like centralization or a new marketplace direction? A new manager or team member, because they don't know how "good" it used to be. Maybe its because they don't know any better, or maybe they are able to see the big picture and see the new change as an opportunity and have the right mindset. That's how my manager acted after she met me.

So ask yourself:

▷ How do I feel about the organization I work for?

▷ Has it been good to me, fair, and for the most part made all good decisions?

▷ How do I feel about the boss I am supposed to serve?

▷ Has he or she always done the right thing, even when I did not see it that way?

▷ Do I trust him or her?

▷ Do I believe in him or her?

If you answered no to these questions, then you have bigger issues than dealing with change or leading through uncertainty; you have a job or career issue, and you need to find a new place to work.

If you answered yes, then you must believe that the biggest changes are like the smaller ones we face every day—that these decisions your organization and leaders are making is in the best interest for everyone. Your job is to focus on how you serve and lead through the change. Be the teacher of the future, not the student left behind in the class of the past.

The Leaders—Coaching Down

Own the change. As followers leading in the middle, your job during uncertain times is to be the one person your boss and organization can count on to secure success no matter what uncertainty or obstacles you face. You will identify how to move forward!

In business, much like in life, we have marching orders ,and sometimes we get to give input and sometimes we just have to say, "Yes ma'am." The key is to know the difference and respond accordingly.

The Power Is in Owning the Decision, Not Empathy

The greatest mistake leaders in the middle make when leading through change is to soften the blow of the change using sympathy. Followers don't need empathy or sympathy. They need confident, strong direction. As a leader, I would rather go the wrong direction confidently than go the right direction with doubt and hesitation. U-turns don't scare me. In fact, I expect them. Only doubt and fear to act guarantee bad decisions or make the movement forward too slow—or fail.

As a leader in the middle, you must coach your teams to be the best version of themselves they can be. Not asking for their input does not mean you do not care or do not value their opinions or expertise. It means their expertise will be needed and appreciated further along in the process. Again, the key is to move forward in delivering on the "how." If you have coached your people well, they will trust you, follow you, and achieve any task you ask them to do (within legal bounds). If not, maybe you don't want those people on your team.

CHAPTER 12

Remember: Only "How" People Allowed

Serving up to those you serve or follow does not mean you must be a "yes man" or "yes woman" or a "suck-up." It means you get paid to do a job, and your job is to do it. You have a few choices:

▷ Take money and do the work better than anyone else if you are comfortable.

▷ Make a decision to see if input is an option if you are uncomfortable.

▷ Decide to move on if you can't align your beliefs and goals with theirs.

Keep in mind, however, there is no correlation between serving up and limiting imagination, individuality, and self-empowerment. To truly serve up during uncertain times, leaders in the middle must be creative and adaptive. The ability to execute during these times is most likely unknown or unproven. These leaders must not be afraid to fail, make a mistake, or to ask too much from their teams. The key is to ask: What is your intent during times of change or any time you are leading? Serve up or suck up.

For leaders in the middle, belief, humility, and commitment must remain consistent in uncertain times.

Leading through change—be it in the workplace or marketplace, and no matter how big or small—and the uncertain times that follow fall into the worn-out phrase of "simple but not easy." Best to keep the Serenity Prayer in mind: *God grant me the serenity to accept the things I cannot change, the courage to change the things I can, and the wisdom to know the difference.*

You can change how you respond. You can change what you do to make sure you end up where you want to be. You just need to change your mindset first.

Final Considerations: Serving and Coaching in Uncertain Times

What change are you facing: Technology? Competition? Economic conditions? Don't answer that. Have you been paying attention? It's a trick question! Get past the "what" and the "why" and focus on the "how."

Succeeding in change is like running a NASCAR pit crew. The faster they can change the tires, add more gas, and do whatever else they do to the car, the faster your car gets back on the track to compete and win.

Don't get caught up proving why you're right and others are wrong. Scarcity and chaos result from that. Just look at Washington, DC. Nothing gets done because no one wants to do anything more than prove the other side wrong. That does not lead to abundance and change. That does not come from a culture of serving up and coaching down and listening to move, learn, and execute. It leads to stopping, defending, and impeding progress.

PART 4

Bridging the Knowledge Gap

Here's a familiar tale: Companies look to implement something new in the business, such as a new technology or software, or a new management or reporting tool. This requires leaders and their teams to attend programs or workshops to learn what they need to do to implement the change and . . . they fail to do so. They may have tried to, even wanted to. But six months, six weeks, six *days* later, it's gone. What happened to all that knowledge? It fell into the "knowledge gap": The space between knowing what to do and *doing* it.

Why this happens comes down to three things: a lack of will, lack of skill, and lack of coaching needed to create high-intensity environments and sustain them. Leaders in the middle with serve up/coach down mindsets can address all these things to bridge the knowledge gap.

CHAPTER 13

The Knowledge Gap Is the Black Hole of Greatness

I was catching up with a former client who had taken a job at another company a few months prior. When we last spoke, he and the other senior leaders had been sent to a training on a new database management system the company said would transform the business. It sounded like a good tool, and I knew he and the other leaders had been looking forward to learning it. But I pretty much knew what would happen next.

So, did you do that training you told me about a few months ago?

"Yeah, Nathan, it was good!"

Did you implement what you learned?

"Yeah, man, right away. It changed our business immediately!"

Do you still do it?

"Nah."

When I tell this story from the stage, everyone laughs. They all say it sounds like their companies. Then, they start to cry. Because it sounds like their companies. In fact, the number one complaint of my clients is their inability to execute on and sustain knowledge they have learned: "It's one and done." "We do the training and then we never hear about it again." "The training is just an act of compliance that everyone forgets when the leaders stop caring about it."

I experienced this when I became a director at a Fortune 100 company and the president rolled out a new employee ranking system. I had no idea how this was going to work, so I sought out a more senior peer and asked. He looked at me with a wide grin and said, "Kid, don't worry about it. In couple of weeks, this idea will fade and go away like all the other great ideas we were going to implement." He was right; within six months the new employee ranking system was never spoken about again.

So how do we keep the systems or processes we implemented from going away in months or even weeks? The answer is to bridge the knowledge gap and make what you learned a sustainable part or principle of your business, which is a lot easier to say than do. Most people in business today know what they *should* do to be successful, but they fail to actually *do* it. That's the bad news: Everyone has this problem. The good news is that leaders in the middle can completely own this problem by serving up and coaching down. But they must understand the root cause of the gap—in others *and* themselves—before trying to bridge it. And that starts with one question: *Does the knowledge gap exist because of a lack of will or a lack of skill or both?*

Lack of Will or Lack of Skill?

Simply put, if leaders in the middle and their people don't have the will and skill to bridge the gap, then they are going to fall into it time and again. With the serve up/coach down mindset in place, however, they accept responsibility to understand this and focus on what the problem is: As a leader in the middle, your job is to understand that lack of will is when someone knows they should do something and has the skill to do it but chooses not to execute. Although this is a choice, it's not necessarily an act of defiance. It may be a perceived lack of benefit (conveyed by the actions of the leaders' bosses) versus the effort required to execute.

As a leader in the middle, your job is to understand that lack of skill is when someone executes on the knowledge—that is, has the will—but fails, because of experience, lack of practice, or just being in the wrong job.

But before leaders in the middle determine which area (or both) their employees fall into, they must first find out which one they themselves fall into. This step toward self-awareness is humbling but awesome for growth as a leader. I know it is always easier to turn the spotlight on our people, but put on your big girl or boy pants and ask yourself: Do I have the will I demand of my people, coach them on the skills they need to develop, and hold all of us accountable to sustaining the changes we are making? Most leaders will discover the answer is "no," and they have failed to realize that they may be the cause of the problems.

Remember: As is the case with any change, sustaining it requires taking the time to coach and keep getting better. And the change starts with determining if there is a lack of will.

CHAPTER 14

Lack of Will

How many times have you gone to a keynote, left with three pages of notes and inspiration, and two days later, you couldn't find those notes (or the inspiration) with a GPS? If you're like most leaders, the answer is "most of the time." That's why when I do a keynote, I spend the first half on mindset, starting with belief. I could teach an audience the greatest business tricks and reveal *the* secrets to success. They could have the right attitude about everything I say and think the content is great. They could be very disciplined in their workplace habits. But if they don't *believe* in what I'm asking them to do, then they won't implement it, let alone sustain it.

Nothing happens if you don't believe in what needs to be executed. Think back to what we covered in Part 3 and leading through change and uncertainty. The success of those changes started with leaders in the middle serving up by believing in their bosses and that the changes were necessary, important, and right. Only then could those leaders coach down to drive the successful execution of that change through their teams and the entire organization.

The same is true with any new knowledge that leads to changes big or small: *Belief equals will and is the first line of attack in bridging the knowledge gap. Our belief determines our conviction. Our conviction keeps us focused on going from knowledge to execution.*

That goes for this entire book, not just this part. Most likely, if you are reading this book, you wanted new or additional knowledge about leading successfully from the middle using the serve up/coach down mindset. (Or someone told you that you needed that knowledge, and you should listen to them because they are obviously very smart.) But you have to have the will to do it in order to implement it. Will lays the foundation.

What Do I Mean by "Will"?

Will is your desire to fight and win. It's the fuel to your fire. The purpose that drives your mind and body to perform. It's the feeling and energy that makes you sacrifice your time to achieve something great. It's the "I love my job, and no matter my job title, I know I am a part of something bigger and important." Just typing this gets me pumped up and exited.

Yes, I know there are people who feel this will "thing" is BS. That you don't need to have will to do your job; you just do your job. Those are almost always the people making excuses for why things don't get done. Or they say they don't live to work; they live for their families. When I hear people say, "My family is my purpose, not my work," I think, "Sounds good, but that's nothing more than justifying your lack of will at work."

Sure, our families should be our number one priority. There is nothing more important to me than my wife and my kids, followed by my parents, my brothers, and my extended family. But having passion for our work and the will to be the best does not have to come at a sacrifice for our families. Jobs that require a lot of travel and many nights away from home do not mean our families have to suffer. I know moms and dads who travel every week, but when they are home, they give their spouses and kids 100 percent. Even with all their time away for work, they somehow always find the time to get away with their families and make memories that the kids will remember their entire lives. On the flip side, I know moms and dads who are home every night with their kids and still don't spend *time* with them, who are not creating positive memories or creating special connections with those they love.

As leaders in the middle, we can't let our employees use their will for something else like their families—or anything they hold dear—as excuses to not have the will at work. Unfortunately, this is not something a leader in the middle can fix.

Consider the story of one of my managers, Mike. Mike definitely had the skill to do his job, but after I hired him, his results were lacking. He had a great plan and good intentions. But when I called him on his results, all I got were excuses blaming everyone but him. That was my clue that Mike was unwilling to do the activities necessary to execute his plan. He had the skill but lacked the will. I sat down with Mike and I told him exactly that: "The reason you are failing is not your lack of ability but it is your lack of willingness to fight—your lack of will." I went on to tell Mike that I could not change his will, but it was my job as the leader to take will out of the equation. "I can help you with skill, but your will is your decision, and you must know that your decision has consequences. It is up to you to believe in what you are doing and be a part of this team, and you cannot fake it. You must *believe* it."

Simply put, Mike's lack of will was not something I could fix, but it was something I could demand as a leader in the middle. Deciphering this lack of will in team members is critical to coaching a successful team, and it doesn't start with them. *It starts with you.*

Set the "Will Standard"

As I said earlier, most people on a team know what they should be doing to be more successful. That includes you as their leader. If you're not doing what's required to serve up, why should they? Attitude and discipline don't just reflect leadership—will or belief does! Leaders in the middle are ultimately the only ones who determine if their people will be allowed to continue to work at a job they have no will to do. But leaders will tolerate that lack of will if they lack it themselves and just "manage" the team. Just managing the team opens up the black hole of the knowledge gap.

Whatever knowledge you are trying to implement and whatever you are doing to coach your team—setting expectations, scrimmaging, holding one-on-ones, doing ride days—won't work unless you have the will to set standards *and* the will to follow through on them. It doesn't do any good to give your team expectations on Monday, expect them to give them to their people by Wednesday, and lack the will to follow through with coaching them.

Why would you expect your managers to commit to one-on-ones with their team members and to sustain that discipline (or any discipline you require) if you lack the will to serve up/coach down and do those things yourself?

When it comes to setting standards as a leader in the middle, I think about raising my children. I refuse to accept any of my children saying, "I did not have time to do my homework" or "I didn't have time to study and bombed the test." Studying is expected, and homework gets done no matter what. I expect commitment to their schoolwork and demand results. I want them to be accountable for their success. But what if, as part of my expectations, I committed to sitting down with my daughter to work on things she was struggling with or quiz her on problems for tests, and then I never found the time? What message does it send her if I lack the will to demand I commit to the standards I set for myself as her dad? I can't be surprised if some of what she needs to learn falls into the knowledge gap.

The same is true in sports. Professional athletes must have the will to work out several times a day, eat right, practice, learn the team's system, and push themselves to learn more and get better. Even superstars need to do this to keep their jobs. If they don't, the coach lets them go. But if the coach fails to set the standards—develop systems to win, instill belief in those systems, and demand their leaders and thus all the players commit to learning them—then the team loses focus. Because the coach lacked the will to do his jobs first and set the standards, which led to the team's lack of will to commit to what they needed to do to win. Even if the team keeps winning, the culture becomes toxic and failure is usually inevitable, at least in the short term until the coach is fired and they reclaim their will to get better.

Just like parents and coaches, leaders in the middle must serve up and coach down with the intent to make our team members the best they can be by displaying the will to do it themselves: Set the standard of serve up/coach down activity and behavior that everyone (including you as the leader in the middle) must do every day, every week, and every month and apply those same standards to any knowledge required.

If you or anyone on the team fails to live up to those standards, ask yourself: Is this a lack of will? Are you or the person *not willing* to do the work, or do you or they *not know how* to do the work?

If the answer is, "Yes, I lack the will," reread this section before continuing to the next one and think about how you might be the cause of your problems. Understand if you have a lack of will before pointing a finger at your bosses and your people.

If the answer is, "Yes, we or they lack the will," continue reading to find out why. When you do, you will usually find you or your people—especially your best people—who lack the will lost it along the way.

If the answer is, "Yes, we do not know how to do the work," then continue reading to the end of this chapter to understand how critical the coach down mindset is.

You've Lost that Willing Feeling

Many people who don't have the will had it at one time and then stopped striving to learn more, because they think they have enough or have done enough. Leaders in the middle must see this in themselves and/or others, understand why it happened, and most importantly, mandate things change. There are two common reasons people lose their will:

1. They feel unchallenged.
2. They feel unappreciated.

When it comes to not feeling challenged, the solution is often not what most leaders in the middle think. It's not about finding a new job. It's about finding a new reason to be better at the one they have first. It's about going back and keeping score. If they can't find that reason, then the only thing left is to find a new job.

When it comes to lacking appreciation, the problem is also often addressed incorrectly with a new incentives or rewards program. Neither are correct. There's nothing wrong with them per se, but they are about goal-setting, not appreciation. The number one requirement for us humans to feel truly appreciated and successful is to have a sense of significance. We crave feeling significant in this world and in our work.

As I have covered in my previous books, appreciation starts with gratitude on the part of the leaders and the organization, which is less common than you might think. I mean, when was the last time you just said a genuine "thank you" to your team without a setup for anything else? After gratitude, feeling significant is about being valued and appreciated and feeling that your efforts matter. When we are no longer appreciated or feel taken for granted, we start to feel insignificant and lose the will to serve or coach—or do anything more than check the box. As a leader in the middle, we must be able to see this and be prepared to resolve it.

We will cover this more in the chapters ahead, but for now, please also realize that people who are not willing to do what they know they should do are not necessarily bad people. They may have made a choice that the reward or result is not worth the sacrifice to achieve it and thus don't feel it has significance for them.

The Reward Must Be Worth the Sacrifice

The only way to be consistent in fueling the will to do the lessons we know we should do is to believe in the "reward" for our work. People have called this reward different things. Simon Sinek calls it our "why," or purpose. In *Start with Why*, he shows how people do more of the "what" when they have the "why." Rory Vaden in *Take the Stairs* describes it as the difference between walking across a long narrow plank on the ground and one suspended in the air; on the ground it's no problem, but high in the air, the consequences make it seem impossible. Vaden notes if you were a parent and you had to cross that narrow plank to save your child, then you would not give it a second thought.

Sinek and Vaden in different ways are pointing out the absolute importance of the reward being worth the work. Again, this is not the same reward we mean when we talk about reward programs. It is the fire that drives you and makes all the hard work worth it. It's what gives you the will to go on and keep serving and coaching through the bad times as well as the good. For some people it might be money, but while money may be a short-term reward, it rarely sustains our will.

Explaining this was actually how I wrapped up my conversation with Mike. I told him that if he did not see that the reward was worth the effort then he should find a place other than my team or our company where he could find his will. Which is what he decided to do not long after we spoke. I saw him a few years later and he actually thanked me for what I did. "Although I hated you for it at the time," he said, "I found my will to be great and a job that gives me that fuel." I don't think Mike will ever send me a Christmas card, but I am grateful that I was able to help him help himself.

Serve Up/Coach Down Mindset: Lack of Will

Remember: Lack of will is a choice based on what we are willing to do to achieve our goals or to do our jobs at and above what is required. As leaders, we can only coach people on the skills if they have the will to learn and do what it takes. No will = No great results. Only when everyone has the will to succeed can a leader in the middle determine if there is a lack of skill leading to the knowledge gap that can be addressed through coaching or training.

The wrong mindset fueled by poor coaching and an inability to serve up: I don't believe it, therefore I don't execute on it. I go through the motions and check the box.

I don't believe the reward is worth the sacrifice, so I make excuses for not believing it and coaching my team on how to execute on the knowledge we have been given.

The correct mindset fueled by great coaching and an ability to serve up: To serve up, my job is to make my team better and help my boss and organization achieve their goals. When it comes to the knowledge gap, I must appreciate and value the investment the organization and leaders made in acquiring knowledge to do that and have the will to act on implementing that knowledge. I must coach my employees to see this and demand that they make a choice to find the will to use that knowledge or find the door.

CHAPTER 15

Lack of Skill

Unlike lack of will, lack of skill or ability is fixable by a strong leader in the middle. But while it is fixable, it's one of the tougher issues for leaders in the middle to understand and commit to solving because of how leadership has been done in corporate America for so long. Here the coach down mindset is essential because while anyone can choose to have the will, leaders in the middle choose to develop the skills. If you're managing your team or protecting them, you're not addressing the lack of skill and the knowledge gap by developing the team and demanding results. And if you're demanding results by saying, "I hire professionals and I expect them to know how to do their job," that's a complete cop-out and justification for not taking the time to coach and invest in your team members. That's like pushing a kid into the deep end of the pool without floaties and yelling, "Better learn to swim!"

The question is: Which leader in the middle are you and will you be?

Are you a leader in the middle who is quick to identify people who are struggling and demand they start doing the hard stuff and delivering results "or else"? Demanding down is the right idea but the wrong mindset. When leaders in the middle have high expectations and demand accountability to results without coaching, they create environments of high tension.

High-Tension Environments: High Expectations + High Level of Activity + Accountability

Are you a leader in the middle who uses a serve up/coach down mindset to develop the skills you and your team need? Leaders in the middle who coach down know their primary job is to make their people better and that time and knowledge are required to develop those skills. The power in addressing the lack of skill is the ability and commitment from the leader to be a coach and to teach and develop skills through practicing and scrimmaging. When leaders in the middle have high expectations and demand accountability and then teach or coach team members how to achieve those expectations as well as hold them accountable to do so, they create environments of high intensity:

High-Intensity Environments: High Expectations + *Coaching* + High Level of Activity + Accountability

That's right: The only difference in creating high-intensity and high-tension environments is the absence of one ingredient: coaching. Not managing, not training, but *coaching* the skills needed to bridge the knowledge gap and succeed. It's the most important ingredient in the recipe.

Like sugar in my favorite cookie, without coaching the flavor changes for the worse. There is no sweet buzz.

High-Intensity Versus High-Tension Environments

Every organization wants this high-intensity buzz—the energy you feel when people are making things happen, having fun, feeling good, and are successful. Morale is high. If this sounds impossible, just look around your office. Although very few organizations have that buzz overall, there are always teams, divisions, or offices that have it. I call them pockets of greatness. And in the middle of those pockets are strong leaders in the middle coaching down and serving up.

High tension is felt just as abundantly as high intensity, but the air is thick with stress not buzz. Any buzz is not from people jumping up and down celebrating but quickly ducking into a cubicle to avoid running into the boss. Morale and energy are as low as the whispers of everyone complaining. People may look like they are doing a lot—and sometimes they are—but the activity equates to low results. They are doing just enough to not get yelled at. And they are certainly not implementing any new knowledge. They stick to the familiar and comfortable and let everything else fall into the gap.

So how do we create environments of high intensity and add the ingredient of coaching?

Consider the following scenario. The leader of an insurance agency team (though honestly this could be any leader in any business) asks each of his employees to call forty customers over the next two weeks to let them know their insurance premiums are going up next month. They need to convince 50 percent of those customers not only to stay with the agency but also to agree to come to the office and meet with the agency. If the employees can't achieve this goal, then the agency will lose more than 50 percent of their business and need to reduce the number of employees or replace them with people who *can* achieve those results.

That's a difficult scenario for any team in any business and the situation might be tense, but it is not a high-tension or a high-intensity environment . . . yet. Only when a leader adds another step in this scenario—to coach the employees on *how* to do this—does the environment become one or the other.

If the leader walks out of the room after explaining the situation and over the following weeks offers no more than a beat down each time they fail, reminding them what is at stake, then it becomes high tension. That saps them of their will to act.

If the leader scrimmages conversations, helping his people find and use the right words and understand how to listen to the customer and empathizes with their situations then the environment begins to become high intensity. Lack of will is not an issue.

As the environment stays high intensity over the following weeks, the leader must then continue to take the time to coach, making the team a little better, improving their skills each time so the employees no longer fear the high expectations and activity. In fact, they start to thrive because of it. The accountably actually makes them better.

When people are pushed beyond what they see as ordinary or what they think they can do and start seeing success from their actions, there is a sense of accomplishment and appreciation in the air and the BUZZ starts to form.

How does this skill story apply to the knowledge gap? Well, consider that same scenario, and let's say that the leader in the middle wanted the team to use a simple social business software to record their interactions with the customers and as a forum for further coaching and learning. The leader arranges for a training on the software immediately after he makes the announcement and says he will be using it constantly to provide feedback. High-intensity environments welcome this knowledge. The people in them see knowledge that comes from coaching down as important and use it to improve their skills and serve up. High-tension environments never welcome this knowledge. The leader just expects the teams to learn it themselves. Before long, the knowledge falls into the gap.

Of course, leaders in the middle coaching employees on the "how" of an expected activity or knowledge does not guarantee environments of high intensity. However, *not* coaching them almost always creates high-tension environments. As leaders we all want our employees to be as committed to the business, the company, and the customer as much as we are. To do this, we must first be committed to the employees and the environments we create.

Tomorrow when you walk into your office, ask yourself and others what they feel: the buzz or the tension?

Not Everyone Can Be a Baseball Player

Note that high-intensity environments do not improve the skills of everyone. Leaders in the middle will inevitably find some employees are not in the right positions or lack the serve up mindset to implement the knowledge or activity. Some employees in high-intensity environments will reveal themselves as lacking the will to implement knowledge and do the jobs required. Those people must find jobs they have the will for. Some employees will show they have the will but lack the ability to develop the skills or right attributes to grow and be successful. It's the job of the leader in the middle to address these situations.

Sometimes, that mindset can even sabotage the knowledge to create a gap. For example, the vice president of a finance company I worked with implemented a new customer data management tool that looked nothing like the current one the company used. One of his leaders in the middle said he got it and was ready to use it. But really, he wasn't. As the vice president later found out, every opportunity that leader had to undermine the tool, he seized it. He told his team that any time they found the software made their job harder than the old software to send him a note. He promised to compile a list and get it to the vice president to get the old software back. In other words, he spent his time trying to prove that the new knowledge the company was trying to implement was the wrong knowledge and shoved it into the gap. Then he blamed the gap he created for why the team failed to implement the software.

But don't think the leader in the middle was completely to blame for his actions. The vice president had told the leader to implement the software, but he never mandated the will to do it. He never coached the leader or the team after the leader left his office. By lacking the will and mandating the development of the skill, the vice president was complicit in creating the knowledge gap.

As leaders in the middle, we must remember that not everybody is great at everything. Not everyone can overcome a lack of skill and be great at what they're doing—or different than what they are doing. Michael Jordan may have been the greatest NBA player in history, but when he retired the first time and tried to make it in baseball, he never made it beyond the minors. He had every talent and attribute that fit the skill sets of his job in the NBA, but that didn't translate to the baseball diamond, no matter how hard he worked. Or consider me: You can try to teach me everything about being an accountant, but regardless of your teachings, I will most likely fail. Accounting columns, rows, and numbers do not excite me in the least. I found my gift on the stage and working with people to make them better leaders. I have passion, a skill set, and attributes to thrive doing those things. I seek knowledge about them. And I have the will to keep developing the skills it takes to be successful doing them.

Serve Up/Coach Down Mindset: Lack of Skill

High intensity is often referred to as "the buzz around the office." When you coach the skills and disciplines needed to meet expectations and develop your team members to their fullest potential, any knowledge that can help the team do that is not only welcome but committed too. Because your team wants to serve up, you can demand down and mandate a commitment as a result of your coaching investments to make them better.

The wrong mindset fueled by poor coaching and an inability to serve up: I create high-tension environments by demanding high activity, having high expectations, and requiring accountability but not coaching my team to develop the skills they need to succeed. Instead, I go through the motions and check the box, or blame anyone or anything, sometimes even maliciously, to undermine the knowledge and create a gap.

The correct mindset fueled by great coaching and an ability to serve up: To serve up, my job is to make my team better and help my boss and organization achieve their goals. I must take responsibility to create high-intensity environments and coach my team to use their skills to generate a return on the investment in the knowledge by the company. I remove any excuses so there is no blame on timing, marketplaces changes, staffing, or the knowledge itself for creating the knowledge gap.

CHAPTER 16

Maintaining the Bridge

When I bring coaching and leadership programs into an organization, I get asked about return on investment: "How will we measure ROI? What kind of tests do you do so we can assess the success of your program?" The organization is looking for what most training companies offer to demonstrate their effectiveness. To show their results, they test the employees. These tests reveal how many people remember what they learned, say they are doing what needs to be done, and lay out what work still needs to be done.

There's a word I want to use to describe these tests, but I won't say it in polite company. Let's just say they're crap. When a company asks me what kind of tests I do, I say, "None." The test of my success is in helping a company bridge the knowledge gap to lead and coach better, which is not found on a piece of paper. *Look for it in real life!* If we implement something in January and we don't hear the words and find people doing the activities that I trained them on in June, it didn't work.

So how do we go from having the will and skill and creating a high-intensity environment to sustaining greatness? *By making knowledge a discipline.*

Old Habits Die Hard

Remember: Humans are creatures of habit. We prefer the comfort of the status quo to disruption. We like change when it makes things more convenient as consumers like Uber or Amazon but hate it when it makes us uncomfortable. In my experience, only about 1 percent—the real doers in an organization—can implement knowledge right away and sustain it. Almost everyone else has or continues to fall outside this category of employees and leaders, including me at one time. Does this mean most people are losers and should be fired? Some, but most should not. They are simply doing less than they are capable of doing or willing to do because they have not learned to serve up and coach down to overcome a lack of will or lack of skill, create a high-intensity environment, and then sustain that knowledge.

Leaders in the middle can do everything right to bridge the knowledge gap by serving up and coaching down, but without a change in behavior, they will end up where they started months later. This is true even at the companies whose trainers' tests showed the company was implementing the knowledge because the tests measured the employees' knowledge after each training showed improvement. But there is no a written test for execution—for showing what the people did to bridge the knowledge gap.

Think you're an exception and part of the 1 percent? Ask yourself these questions: Have you never known you should be doing something better or with more discipline and didn't? Have you ever changed your behavior and then stopped changing, justifying stopping it with a rationalization, excuse, or blame of someone or something? If your answer is no, congratulations! The rest of you should do the following exercise before continuing:

▷ Write down three things you know you should be doing as a leader in the middle that you are not committed to doing today.

▷ After you write your list, give it to your boss, a mentor, or someone whom you trust to hold you accountable and ask them to do exactly that: hold you accountable over the next ninety days to doing those three things, no excuses.

▷ If it works, add three more, and do it again and again until you run out of three things.

▷ If it doesn't work, reread this part of the book and ask yourself if you really have the will to be doing what you are doing and get better as a leader in the middle by serving up and coaching down.

Final Considerations:
The Knowledge Gap

The knowledge gap is a real issue and all the ensuing out-comes, good and bad, are the results of the leader in the middle's decisions and actions. Next time you face this gap in business or life, ask yourself: Is it a lack of will or lack of skill? Lack of will is a choice, and allowing lack of will is never the right choice. Lack of skill requires the commitment of the "player" and the "coach" to get better at what they do.

Some people have the ability and skill but don't have the will and discipline. Mandate it all or mandate they quit. No one likes to work hard and feel like they are failing. The harsh thing is to allow people to remain in this state of self-destruction. The selfless thing to do is to empower them to match their will with their skills and help them find personal success elsewhere.

The knowledge gap is only present when someone decides not to execute and a leader decides to accept it. To achieve great success in anything, success only comes when you believe in what you're doing and see the reward to be worth the sacrifice you must make to achieve it.

Return on investment is not in how much the employees know but how much they continue to do in the weeks, months, and year ahead. *That* is your serve up mindset. The company spent money for the keynote or training to get this knowledge. Everyone agrees it is important. Your job as the leader in the middle is to make sure that everyone on the team continues to believe and changes their behavior to make the knowledge a sustainable part of a high-intensity environment.

PART 5

Choosing Time Management

I get several requests each year to do presentations and workshops on time management. I'm sure more would ask me but just don't have the time to reach out. This is amusing but true—and sad given that for generations countless experts across all media have discussed how to manage time. So what's the deal? The deal is we don't need a new system for managing time. We need a different mindset. Because time management isn't a skill problem, it's a will problem.

Simply put, too many leaders in the middle choose to not use their time wisely. The key word is "choose." In order to serve and coach effectively, leaders in the middle must choose to prioritize the most important serving and coaching tasks. When they identify and commit to their top priorities—differentiating between what they must do and what is urgent—they will end up with fewer problems and more time.

Anyway, I know you're crunched for time, so let's get going. To speed things up, I even chose to cut this part down to three chapters.

CHAPTER 17

Get Your Priorities Straight

What if I were your boss and presented you a four-year plan in which I wanted you to go on 5,040 appointments that were about forty-five minutes long each. What would you say? That's 1,260 per year, 105 per month, or seven per day in addition to any other work you have to do. Would you say, "Sure, Nathan, that sounds totally reasonable and not crazy at all!" and then leave, no questions asked? Or would you stare at me in total disbelief, mutter under your breath, "You're nuts," and think about where to send your résumé when you get back to your desk?

Chances are you lean toward the latter. Most people do when I ask them. But if you did, then next time you hear a teenager complain about all they have to do in high school—you know, the ones we call spoiled, entitled, and lazy?—you'd better think twice before responding. The number of appointments I just laid out is what we ask the average high school student to do over four years in terms of classes. Only we expect them to complete those appointments in only 180 days (the length of most school years), or thirty-six weeks.

Here's the math: The average number of class periods in a school day is seven: 7 classes x 180 days x 4 years = 5,040 appointments.

And that's in a six-hour day *with* forty-five minutes for lunch! I'm giving you fifty-two weeks and (even if you just work nine to five) a minimum of two extra hours on the clock to complete the same amount of appointments and do all your other work. Okay, fifty weeks if you take vacation. That's still an extra fourteen weeks and ten hours a week. Still think it's impossible to manage? Well, the solution isn't to move back in with your parents but to shift your mindset about how to schedule time and prioritize what you must do as a leader in the middle.

We don't afford our kids the choice to go to high school and do what they need to do. We must do the same and choose to prioritize the activities of coaching and serving to manage our time better.

Lack of Priorities

What do you hear when someone says, "I want to work smart, not hard." My Millennial son's high-school friends say this all the time. What they mean, of course, is they want to work less and get paid more, not make more time in the day to get things done. But I'm not just dumping on Millennials here. My experience is this phrase has become the ultimate justifier for people of any age who want to do less. Working smart should be about getting sixty hours of results from forty hours of work, not doing as little as possible while "working" forty hours a week and still keeping your job.

Working smart comes down to one thing: owning your priorities and making smart choices. Most leaders know this, yet even the smartest of us fail to do this. My kids were Harry Potter fans, and I always think of Hermione Granger (the smart witch) when I say this. In the first movie, she yells at Harry and Ron Weasley, "I hope you're pleased with yourselves. We could all have been killed. Or worse, expelled." To which Ron replies, "She needs to sort out her priorities." So do you.

Simply put, a lack of (or unclear) priorities is the number one contributor to a leader's time management problems. But in all fairness, it's easy to confuse priorities as leaders in the middle. What do you do first: Serve the boss and do the report she just asked for? Deal with the customer who needs our attention or that client whose deal is falling apart? Get those employee reviews that HR needs *now*? Push all those things off and hold my weekly one-on-one with my top performer? Any of the other countless urgent and important things on my to-do list? The list of urgent and important things on a leader in the middle's to-do list is always overwhelming and always has been. This is why Stephen Covey and hundreds of other experts have tried to help us sort out what we mean by "urgent" and "important." So why do we continue to fail at getting on top of those to-do lists? It's not only in understanding the difference between important and urgent but also understanding what we must do to lead and prioritize as a leader in the middle.

The important tasks you don't do lead to bigger problems long term and the inability of your team or you to handle them quickly and efficiently.

What Do I Mean by "Important"?

In case you have never covered this before or need a refresher on definitions, let me lay out the difference between "important" and "urgent" tasks. Note: Although some tasks can be urgent *and* important and thus essential to deal with immediately, more than 99 percent of all tasks fall into these categories:

> ▷ *Important tasks* are proactive activities we need to do in order to develop our business, our people, and ourselves. They are almost always designed to lead to positive results and getting better at what we do.

> ▷ *Urgent tasks* are usually the result of things that are happening to us or our teams as a result of problems or requests, and thus, reactive. Not all urgent tasks are negative—some are immediate opportunities that are great—but even those can become negative when they get in the way of what is really important.

Whereas the consequences of not doing the important tasks are much greater than not doing the urgent ones, leaders in the middle choose to prioritize the urgent ones because of the nature of those consequences:

▷ The consequences of not doing important tasks are devastating but rarely result in any immediate short-term pain. The damage may not be felt for weeks, months, even years. The work they require takes weeks to take effect so leaders in the middle put them off.

▷ The consequences of not doing the urgent tasks are often not as devastating in the long term as important ones, but the pain is more pronounced and immediate. Humans prefer comfort over pain, so leaders in the middle tend to focus on those urgent tasks, no matter how small they are.

What we choose to do when faced with these consequences is why time management is a will issue, not a skill issue. It's not *how* we deal with the tasks and consequences or *what* we do, but choosing to make the important or urgent a lower priority. Leaders in the middle too often go for the urgent. After all, they're urgent, right?

I've had countless leaders in the middle tell me that they can't do all their coaching activities—one-on-one meetings, ride days, scrimmages—because everyone is always busy handling some problem. And therein lies the problem: *Solving a problem, dealing with a situation, or checking a box by completing an urgent task instead of focusing on an important one can undermine leaders in the middle, even as things are getting done.*

Lack of an Important Focus Can Create Urgent Consequences

Let's consider what I mean from a "serve out" perspective, and a task I think we all can agree is important: keeping customers updated. Of course, everyone loves calling customers with good news. Who wants to sit on news that will make everyone feel good? Once we are sure the good news is ready to share, we make sharing it the most urgent and important thing on our list. The opposite is true too: Whereas most of us hate calling customers with bad news, we know we have to. Unless the consequences are immediate and severe, we might try and solve the problem or at least get a solution in motion before contacting the customer, but we can't hide the news. We know the task is urgent and important, and we have to do it.

But what about when there is no news to share? Whether you think the phrase "No news is good news" is true or not, no news is only good news if you give it. No news is lazy behavior if you use it as an excuse for not calling customers. "But Nathan, I had nothing new to share so it wasn't necessary to call, right?" Wrong. Think about how you felt when you were waiting for news on something big to you: a home loan, tickets for the show your kids wanted for Christmas, a delivery that might not arrive in time. The longer you go without knowing anything, the more your thoughts turn to the negative. It becomes harder and harder to have faith and stay positive, even if you trust the people who are working on it.

People hate not being informed. Customers don't mind if you have a lack of news or information, but they hate not knowing that. Not knowing makes them feel unimportant, which is especially bad if they *are* important. That's why I always enforced the "Head on the Pillow Rule" for my leaders in the middle: Your head should never hit the pillow unless you and your team have made and returned all important phone calls, including those "no news" calls: "Hey, just wanted to give you a heads-up that we're still on target but haven't heard anything new. If you have any questions, give me a call, but we're still on it."

We can all agree that calls like this are not urgent, just important, so there are often no immediate consequences. Problem is, by not doing this task, you potentially create immediate urgent problems and tasks:

▷ Upset customers who demand more attention and thus more of your time, affecting other tasks.

▷ Paranoid customers who think something is wrong and want more updates and details of everything that is happening—even threatening to go to the competition unless the "problem" (which doesn't exist but now does in their minds) is fixed.

▷ Annoyed bosses whom you did not serve because they got repeated calls from that customer through the weekend.

Since actions express our priorities, ignoring my pillow rule over time and not calling back customers makes them believe they are not priorities. Keep ignoring it and even the most understanding customers will start complaining of bad customer service—a reputation that spreads quickly in the age of social media. That's a real problem that can't be fixed by a couple of phone calls and may never get resolved. All because the leader in the middle failed to see the consequence of an important task and understand a fundamental rule of all consequences: The longer the delay of the consequence, the larger the impact.

The Justification Trap

What the "Head on the Pillow" rule really avoids is justifying not using our time for the activities of serving up and coaching down. And let's face it, we all look for reasons not to do them. Because important serve/up coach down tasks involve things like studying, practicing, and learning not only lack immediate consequences but also offer little or no immediate gratification. It's easy to say, "Why do it?"

Solving the smallest urgent problems sate our need for immediate gratification. Who doesn't love that sense of accomplishment we get in crossing something off our to-do lists? Even better, I can use those urgent tasks as a justification for not doing the less fun, more difficult important stuff. Fill in the blank with something that happened this past week, and you know exactly what I mean: "Man, I was going to do that very important task, but [fill in the blank] happened today, and I had to jump on it immediately."

All that excuse does is put short-term actions over long-term gains. It's the way leaders in the middle get sucked into the "circle of urgent"—the whirlpool of fires we must put out to seemingly keep our jobs instead of doing the important things that would prevent those fires from spreading in the first place.

I say "seemingly" because those fires always seem worse when you lack perspective. Think back on any fires you put out more than a year ago and ask yourself the following questions: Am I still putting out the same fires and dealing with the same issues that led to them? Are we any better at handling them? If the answers to both these questions aren't enthusiastic yesses, then you are focusing too much on the urgent tasks. You also probably have a morale issue and definitely have a time management issue when it comes to serving up and coaching down.

Serve Up/Coach Down Mindset: Get Your Priorities Straight

Do you make excuses for not meeting your obligations to your boss, your team, and your organization? As in, "I can't find the time to coach because those other tasks are a priority." Then you need to make a choice to make them more important than all the urgent (but not important) tasks on your to-do list. The wrong mindset is always about justifying how *not* to be better. The right mindset is about using your time to prioritize serving up and coaching down to be better.

The wrong mindset fueled by poor coaching and an inability to serve up: I was going to do all those coaching activities, but I got too busy. Everything else demanded my time. People needed me *now, now, now*. So forget what I said about what's important. Let's get this done, and when nothing else is urgent, we'll get back to the one-on-ones and scrimmaging.

The correct mindset fueled by great coaching and an ability to serve up: I know if I am to serve my boss and accomplish what is expected of me, I need to be coaching my employees and make that my number one priority. Coaching activities must be as or more important than urgent.

This brings us to the next chapter, and the one skill you can teach yourself and coach your team on when it comes to time management—as long as you have the will to commit to it: the must-do list.

CHAPTER 18

The Must-Do List

The to-do list is one of the biggest nuisances for a leader in the middle when it comes to coaching. I'm not saying to-do lists aren't important, but they are mostly populated by urgent tasks, not important ones. The longer we procrastinate the things on the list, the more urgent the tasks become. Must-do lists are different. These are lists of important tasks done on a regular basis that have no immediate consequence (so they are rarely urgent), but if not done can have *huge* long-term consequences. So we *must* make them a priority.

What goes on a must-do list? Almost all coaching activities (scrimmaging, weekly one-on-ones, setting expectations for employees, holding employees accountable), as well as your own personal and professional development tasks (telling your family you love them, reading a book, taking a class). Activities for serving across to other divisions or teams and out to customers (like those "no news" calls) should also be on this list. And what about serving up to the boss? Having the will to commit to the must-do list—demanding more of yourself and your people instead of protecting them by saying there isn't enough time to get things done—is the ultimate demonstration of serving up! Getting stuck in our to-do lists is how we get stuck in something I call the "proof factor" and trying to prove all the reasons why not.

Stop trying to prove to your boss that you and your people don't have the time to do what is important and do what you must to get it done.

Three Steps for Creating and Owning a Must-Do List

The first step for leaders in the middle in creating a must-do list is not the list itself but owning their calendars, which is a lot harder than it sounds. The process requires three things—the same three things required to bridge the knowledge gap:

1. **Mindset:** Enhancing your mindset to accept that you own your time and commit to do the work.

2. **Discipline:** Writing out your priorities, adding them to your calendar, demanding this from those that report to you, and sharing it with those you serve up to.

3. **Execution:** Not accepting any excuses from yourself or your team, staying committed to

your important tasks, and fighting the need to drop them to do the urgent ones.

You will find that executing your must-do list as a leader in the middle is more work at the start, but after a few months, the results far outweigh the lack of short-term benefits. You will find that you are working on daily activities that are in alignment with your long-term goals. That your time management issues are no longer an issue of time, rather an issue of priorities and discipline to keep the urgent at bay. You will also find fewer urgent problems, because coaching down leads to better anticipation and resolution of those problems to eliminate or mitigate their effects in the future.

The second step for leaders in the middle in creating must-do lists is creating the list of priorities. So take a moment right now to write down your priorities as a leader in the middle.

Here's a sample list I created based on my experience with thousands of leaders in different industries. Feel free to add in specific tasks for your industry as long as they are important. Be aware that the more you add, the more difficult focusing on and prioritizing the tasks becomes.

Coaching Down and Developing Employees

▷ Weekly practice meeting with the team.

▷ Ride days in the field three days per week.

▷ One-on-one development meetings with direct reports.

▷ Inspecting our expectations of our employees.

▷ Holding employees accountable.

Serving Up

▷ Dashboard report to boss to make sure she/he is 100 percent up to date.

▷ Checking in with boss for updates and progress.

▷ Schedule weekly one-on-ones to ensure correct alignment.

▷ Calling any customers with updates even if there is no news.

Building the Business, Team, and Myself

▷ Recognizing employees and sharing with upper management.

▷ Recruiting new talent (in the field two hours per week).

▷ Serve out to handle customer and department issues.

▷ Serve across and meet with other departments and teams (two hours per week).

▷ Personal development: read part of a book every day (or listen to a podcast, read an article, watch videos, etc.).

Once you complete your own list, you can then compare how much time you spent over the past few weeks working on the important tasks versus others and see the gaps that need to be filled. Then you can move to the third step: Don't just ink it, schedule it!

As a leader in the middle, I always found that writing something down on a piece of paper or electronically was not enough to keep me focused on what I had to do. If it was not on my schedule, it wasn't as much of a priority, if only because no one else could see it and hold me to it. If I didn't fill my schedule up with my priorities, it quickly got filled with urgent tasks and other people's priorities.

Remember: The amount of time we have is a constant. The only variable is how we choose to use it. The key to maximizing time as leaders in the middle is to break our schedules up into small blocks that allow for extreme focus on *one* important task at a time. This allows us not only to stick to those tasks that are important but shows the people we coach and the leaders we serve that they are important to us.

Schedule every important task and invite every participant. Set alerts to remind you. Make sure your boss and the rest of the team can see these tasks.

No one is perfect, but keep to these meetings as much as possible, and if you know you will miss one in advance, reschedule before, not after, you miss it. Move it up versus back if you can. If you have to cancel, ask yourself if there is another option first. Technology gives us a lot of options to keep our important commitments.

Okay, I get it. This sounds like another fantasy, right? Even if you *wanted* to do all the coaching activities and agree that if you did them every week you and your people would get better and serve your boss and organization well. But let's talk reality: *Those coaching sessions can be a little boring . . . and we need to handle some real big customer issues right now . . . and by the way the month-end is coming and we have some KPIs that need to be hit (or else), and you want to talk about consequences—let's miss the KPIs!*

Does some or all of that sound familiar? Chances are, as a leader in the middle, you have heard and said something similar. So what do most people do? They say forget the coaching and it's all hands on deck. We need results now! See how easy it is to get trapped in an urgent mindset and sacrifice the important tasks of making your people and our businesses better? Don't sacrifice a serve up/coach down culture by creating one that will lead to time management issues from top to bottom, as well as the development and morale of the entire team. In today's world, there are so many distractions that get in the way of giving coaching down and serving up 100 percent of our attention and focus. Trying to focus on everything at once only enhances those distractions, blurs our vision, and makes everything but the people who matter most our focus. When we learn to schedule our time for them, we not only find that time but also will find we have more of it to use.

Serve Up/Coach Down Mindset: The Must-Do List

The must-do list prioritizes what is important to serve up and coach down. It keeps urgent tasks in balance and at bay.

The wrong mindset fueled by poor coaching and an inability to serve up: Something urgent happens—not a crisis but something perceived or treated that way: Cancel everything. Cancel every important coaching activity because we need boots on the ground to focus on this. We can't worry about being better next time. We need to get the other stuff done this time!

The correct mindset fueled by great coaching and an ability to serve up: In order to get better and be better, I need to focus on what I must do and all the activities that I and my boss know are important. I want and expect to be the best I can be at my job and so does my team. I should never be too busy not to do what I must do to make those things priorities.

CHAPTER 19

A Tale of Two Leaders

Let's end this journey through time management with a story of two leaders in the middle: Mark and Brandon. Mark and Brandon work for the same manufacturing company servicing different products. Both are good guys, manage the same number of people, have tenure at the company, and know the business. Mark's team is in charge of the newer division selling and servicing plastic blocks. He and his team are successful, but he will tell you they need to do more and take on new adventures to be as big as Brandon's division. Brandon's division is in charge of selling and servicing metal blocks, which is more established and has more customers and a stronger financial foundation to manage.

On the surface, it sounds like Brandon has it a lot easier than Mark, right? Not if you ask Brandon, which I did when I started working with them on coaching their teams. Because Brandon has a time management problem and Mark does not.

Brandon's work life is a constant stream of urgent customer and team issues, like the fact that two of his people just quit and his customers' orders are incorrect or delayed. But why coach? Brandon believes if you want a job done right, you have to do it yourself. That's why he is usually the first one in the office, the last one to leave, and comes to work most Saturdays. When he found out one of his team members never returned phone calls, he took the phone and did it himself. As a result, Brandon works very hard and long hours but has no control over his day. Everything is in a state of emergency and crisis. Brandon realizes he has a time management issue. The problem is, he is looking for a time management tool to solve it. He makes no commitment to any of the important tasks of coaching. In fact, he managed to schedule and hold only four practice meetings with his team in the first six months I worked with him and none in the last two. He says he does not have time to schedule one-on-one sessions because he is too busy.

Mark is busy too, but he is a big believer in coaching his employees and being coached. He has a family, and he makes sure each hour in his day is used effectively so he can leave on time to spend time with his wife and two boys. That does not mean Mark works forty hours a week. At his management and compensation level, his job requires sixty to sixty-five hours per week most weeks, yet he still attends most of his kids' events. Because Mark is busy but never *too* busy, because he prioritizes his time and schedules every hour starting at 6:45 a.m. with daily prayer. His calendar is packed with practice meetings with his employees, one-on-one development sessions, quarterly planning sessions, recruiting talent time, and client visits. Mark also makes time to email his boss daily updates and a weekly dashboard report, because he knows his boss wants to know that the business is moving in the right direction. He has chosen to prioritize the important things professionally and personally, made his must-do list, and taken control of his calendar to manage it, avoiding many of the customer and team problems that Brandon constantly deals with.

So which leader in the middle would you want to hire, work for, or be?

Of course, the answer is Mark in most circumstances. If it were my company and I needed to take leave from my company for a month, I'd be comfortable with either of them, maybe even most comfortable with Brandon. He'd make sure that every little unimportant detail was covered. But if I need to grow my business, I'm not asking Brandon. I'm asking Mark. Because that's what Mark was focused on: development and growth.

When I started working with them, Mark seized the nature of important tasks to serve his and Brandon's boss better. Their boss was the owner of the company (one of the best in the business), but he was very difficult to work with and a micromanager. Mark took that as a cue to communicate better and make sure he took the time to tell his boss what was going on by providing those daily and weekly reports the way he wanted them. When their boss asked them to come in to the corporate office for an important meeting, Brandon's first response was: "Why are we having a meeting? Can we do it over the phone? I have too many urgent things to attend to." Mark, however, despite having travel plans to meet with his team, accepted the meeting request with the mindset that if the boss needs to meet then it must be important. He adjusted his schedule, informed his team of the change, and then contacted his boss to see if he needed anything prepared for the meeting.

In the end, Mark and Brandon both showed up, but the difference was their mindset. Brandon resented the meeting while Mark embraced it, just like he embraced the choice to make time for coaching. Brandon said he was open to the same coaching as Mark, but he was too busy to get on top of things by prioritizing what was important. If he had, he easily could have avoided many of the fires he was putting out. For example, Brandon's team missed three deliveries in a week for a product that takes almost a year to deliver. That's right: twelve months from the time the customer orders the blocks to the time that customer receives metal blocks. And yet Brandon's team missed those three deliveries. Of course, that week was chaos for Brandon as he made call after call to the customer, the manufacturer, the shipping team, and the warehouse. He blamed everyone but himself for not being on top of the important tasks and scheduling meetings and coaching activities that might have uncovered issues and breakdowns before they became urgent problems. Tasks Brandon is too busy to start doing now.

Choose Your Mindset

Some of you may be thinking Brandon needed those problems to feel important. Perhaps. But the truth is most successful leaders in the middle are never too busy to take on more and those who struggle are always too busy to do what they are already supposed to do, much less take on more responsibility. The difference is in their choices. The work needs to get done. Leaders in the middle who serve up know they need to choose to find the time by demanding they and the people on their teams maximize their time by focusing on the important tasks and not accepting time management excuses. And here's the thing: After dealing with hundreds of companies over the past fifteen years, I realized that those leaders who prioritized the important tasks always handled the urgent stuff too.

It's not like Mark's team never had any urgent issues. The team just handled them and the important ones too. By taking the time to coach down, Mark empowered his team to be better and more equipped to manage their time to serve him as the leader. Mark's team knew Mark never made excuses, so they knew they could not make them either. This allowed the team to focus on how to complete the important and urgent tasks rather than blame others for why they happened. In fact, by focusing on the important tasks (making the calls they needed to make, going on client visits, staying on top of the entire supply chain) they put out fires like those delivery problems Brandon's team had before they even started.

Your people will always have problems if you accept them. Brandon did; Mark didn't. That meant more time for Mark's team to grow and develop, and when he wasn't traveling, Mark still managed to tuck his kids in at night with a clear conscience while Brandon was still at work.

Simply put, Mark's team reflected his mindset and Brandon's reflected his. The leaders in the middle set the example. Mark's team always found time because Mark did, whereas Brandon's team struggled because Brandon felt he was too busy to do anything but handle those urgent tasks. So he accepted when his people gave the same excuses for being too busy or having problems, and those problems will not just continue, they will multiply along with excuses for why it happened and blame for whose fault it is. And no one will manage to have the time to fix it.

Final Considerations: Time Management

When it comes to time management, the wrong mindset is an unwillingness to change your priorities and stop making excuses. The right mindset is that you can always be better and focus on the things you know are important. You never let the urgent get in the way. This is why time management is a "will" issue. Time management is not a system. Time management is a result of your priorities and your choices and judgment.

Remember: Every coaching activity is about doing things to make your people better. Urgent tasks and checking boxes give you immediate gratification and get things done, but they are an unproductive mindset of busy-ness. All that work comes at the expense of important tasks that lead to better time management that serves your boss and organization, because your team is never too busy to take on more responsibility.

And what happens if a boss gives you contradictory priorities on what is important? The wrong mindset is to attack. The wrong mindset is also to let it go. It's okay to struggle with direction; it's just not okay to *keep* struggling with it. Take the time to make time by asking your boss to coach you on the priorities and sort them out so the work you are doing is in alignment with the long-term goals. But never say what your boss is asking for is unrealistic. If your boss is asking you to do it, you have to choose to make time to do it. If you still think you don't have time, the problem is you.

PART 6

Everyone Is Important, but No One Is Required

In business and in life, we must remember to focus on the number one requirement of humans: the need to feel significant and appreciated. That comes from respect more than rewards and trophies. Yet how are leaders in the middle respecting those who deliver high-performance results and exceed their expectations in the present if they don't demand the same thing of others who have succeeded in the past but have grown complacent? How are they serving their bosses and companies if they aren't constantly pushing the team to get better, including "building a bench" for the future? Yes, everyone needs to feel significant, appreciated, and respected, but no one is entitled to anything; *everyone is important, but no one is required.*

Think that sounds disloyal? It's not. Leaders' loyalty to their people should be based on contribution, not tenure: what they're doing, not what they've done. Leaders in the middle who have a serve up/coach down mindset understand this. Coaching and serving conveys respect and appreciation for everyone they work with and for, and it makes them feel significant. It also holds everyone accountable to high-performance results, including themselves! Because if leaders feel they are too valuable or have earned the right to no longer serve or coach, then they must consider if they are not being accountable to themselves and have lost their will to lead.

CHAPTER 20

What Have You Done for Me Lately? Loyalty Versus Accountability

I was running a coaching workshop for leaders in the middle at a Fortune 50 tech company when a leader raised his hand with a look of genuine concern on his face. We had been discussing recruiting and the importance of "building a bench"—the value of networking, researching, meeting top talent (even bringing them in for interviews), and always looking to add new and better talent to our teams. Most of the leaders nodded their heads in agreement at this concept, but the leader who raised his hand didn't like it at all.

"Nathan," he said, "I understand the need for adding new talent to our teams when we have an opening. But if we are constantly recruiting new people, doesn't that tell our team that they are not important and that we are not loyal to them? I mean, shouldn't we be loyal to them if they are loyal to us?"

I had heard this complaint hundreds if not thousands of times when discussing this topic and was ready with my response: *That depends first on how you define "loyal" and second on how each team member's behavior demonstrates loyalty and affects the success and health of the team.*

"I don't know exactly how I define loyalty, but I want my team to know I am loyal to them, as I expect them to be loyal to me," he replied.

It was exactly the kind of knee-jerk defending up/protecting down response I expected, so I pushed him a little: *If being loyal to your people means that as long as they're succeeding* and *giving their best, we stay loyal to them? Then yes. But please notice I said "and" not "or." The "and" matters, right?* He nodded that he understood, but I wasn't sure he did: *Okay, so what if you have a team member not meeting your expectations but has been with your team longer than anyone else at the company? Do you ignore that because they have earned your trust and loyalty?*

"Maybe. I have some veterans that I don't expect to do the stuff my rookies do."

This was not an unusual response. In Part 3: Serving and Coaching in Uncertain Times, I talked about a leader who said something similar when we discussed holding people to higher standards. In situations like these, I have learned the reason leaders in the middle don't do this has little to do with loyalty and more to do with fear of losing those veterans and having to replace them. (If that does happen, this is why they need to build a bench.) I hoped to make this leader see this as we continued our discussion from the stage:

So you expect your rookies to do important tasks and work that you don't make your veterans do. Let me ask you this, then: If the veterans did that work, would they and the team be more successful?

"Absolutely, but I don't want to micromanage them."

None of this is about loyalty or micromanaging. Loyalty should be based on contribution, not tenure. By justifying it as not wanting to micromanage, you're just making an excuse for not coaching and demanding results from everyone regardless of their tenure. Only when people at any level are succeeding and giving their best—always looking to learn and get better—should they have and expect your loyalty.

What I was telling that leader in the audience and have told hundreds of leaders in the middle before and since is what you must understand right now: Giving your loyalty to people who are not serving you not only damages a team's culture, but also affects the success of those on the team who *are* giving their best and striving to get better. All because you failed to live by an essential leader in the middle principle: Don't confuse loyalty with doing your job and holding everyone accountable to exceeding expectations. Remember: Everyone is important, but no one is required.

Don't Be Loyal to a Fault

There are two types of people who leaders in the middle mistakenly give their loyalty to but whose behavior does not demonstrate loyalty. People they tend to protect, defend, and leave alone because they believe they are unchangeable, uncoachable, untouchable, or it's just too much of a pain in the ass to coach or deal with them:

1. People giving their best but not succeeding
    or getting better.
2. People succeeding but not giving their best
    or getting better.

If people are giving their best but not succeeding, it's actually disloyal to keep them in their positions. In fact, it's downright cruel. Coach them up or coach them out; find a place where their efforts will match their skills and success will match their best.

However, what if they are successful but not giving their best or their most, meaning they are successful in spite of themselves and their efforts? This is a bigger problem for leaders in the middle who must find out why. Is it that they are not being challenged? Feel entitled based on the success they have had after a long tenure at the company? The next stop on that bus is complacency. Before that happens, leaders in the middle must ask themselves why they're accepting less than the best from these people. It doesn't matter if people are achieving success greater than anyone else on the team. They're not achieving the results they should be achieving and being held accountable to that.

Yet chances are the leaders in the middle are not holding those people accountable. They're accepting those results. You know what message that sends the other team members? That their goal should be the same: Be good enough so the boss will not make us try as hard and will leave us alone. So why do we accept this behavior? The reason I shared with the leader in the audience that day is what I have found to be the (yes, *the*) truth about loyalty and accountability: Leaders in the middle use loyalty to benefit them when it is convenient and to avoid conflict and difficult conversations.

Stop Justifying Anyone's Lack of Activity—Including Yours!

In my entire career, I have never met a single leader in the middle who didn't recruit because it was disloyal to his or her team. Simply put, leaders don't recruit because it's disloyal. They don't do it because it's a pain in the ass and hard to do. But you must. As the coach of your team, your job is to build the best team possible and then keep winning, exceeding expectations for your boss and the company. That job includes making your team members better and adding better people when necessary. In sports, if a team wins a championship, that team does not rest on its laurels. When the celebration is over, the question becomes: Do we have the best players in the right positions to win again next year? They draft new players, and most veterans have to earn their jobs the next year. It doesn't matter if that player is the MVP star quarterback from the Super Bowl or the rookie looking to break out. Everyone is important, but no one is required unless they can help the team win again—including the coach!

The same is true in business. "Everyone is important, but no one is required" might sound harsh, but it teaches an essential lesson for leaders in the middle about balancing employee appreciation and employee accountability: It's not about making popular decisions; it's about making the right decisions for the team.

If leaders in the middle want to build thriving, winning cultures, they must serve their customers and bosses with the same vigor and commitment they expect of their employees. They must build the best team possible, which means coaching all their people up or out. They want those they coach to grow in their success every year and if they can't do that, then they want to move them out to somewhere they can.

Loyalty should not be confused with gratitude for a job well done. Leaders in the middle must always be grateful and appreciative for their teams. But loyalty is measured in mental and physical contribution by team members, not time served. We've all had employees who quit years ago but still come to work. Are they deserving of the same loyalty as our superstars? So often in business today, we expect to be judged by what we have done, but our true success and value is based on what we are doing today and keep doing consistently.

It might have once been true that you're only as good as your last success. But in today's world? You're only as good as your current, consistent, and potential future successes. It's "What have you done for me lately?" That mindset should be true for leaders in the middle because it is certainly true for those superstars serving them. They are being loyal to you by giving their best and striving to be better, but that is only as long as you are the best fit for their future. No one wants people to stay with them when an opportunity to be better lies elsewhere. That's how you end up with an employee who will eventually resent you and cares little about being accountable to anyone.

Leaders in the middle must stop being held captive by loyalty and justifying bad behavior to avoid conflict or accepting less than anyone's best. That's not serving up or coaching down. That's maintaining the status quo, which can be hard to break free from.

Serve Up/Coach Down Mindset: Loyalty Versus Accountability

The belief that everyone is important, but no one is required balances loyalty and accountability. It prevents leaders in the middle from being blinded by loyalty and compels them to coach all team members to be successful. That includes building a bench for future success. Leaders in the middle must understand their bosses' and organizations' direction and beliefs and coach those they lead to exceed expectations by giving their best and always getting better.

The wrong mindset fueled by poor coaching and an inability to serve up: I prioritize loyalty above all else! Even if people are succeeding without giving their best or are giving their best without much success, I should stand by them because they are delivering or at least trying to. We're doing fine. There's no need to change.

The correct mindset fueled by great coaching and an ability to serve up: I must mandate everyone I lead give their best, strive to get better, and understand that everyone is important, but no one is required. That includes me! We're all only as good as our current, consistent, and potential future successes.

CHAPTER 21

You Owe Me: Loyalty Versus Tenure

During a break at a corporate event I was leading, I overheard a guy from engineering talking to a newer employee. I had never worked with this guy but knew he had been at the company for more than ten years. He had produced steady and decent results for most of that decade-plus and was among the best at the company. Some had produced better results over that time, but most had left the company while he stayed. And he appeared to be leveraging that for all it was worth. Everything about his words and even his posture screamed "big fish in a small pond" attitude and gave off a "don't mess with me" vibe. Not that he was unlikeable. On the contrary, like most people, I found him funny and charming. But not in this conversation. He told the other employee how the company "lets me do my own thing" and how "bored" he was. I couldn't resist inserting myself into their conversation.

Hey, I couldn't help but overhear you guys talking and what you said. So if you're bored, why don't you find a different job and quit?

"Oh, I couldn't quit. They need me."

They might need you a lot less than you think they do.

"No, they need me."

I decided to push him. *Well, I have to tell you: If you're doing a job you don't want to do and you think they need you more than you need them, then you are probably doing a lot less good stuff than you think. In fact, you're probably disrupting the team.*

I got pulled away to restart the event, so the conversation ended before he could respond. But I told him to find me after we concluded if he wanted to continue talking, which he did. Clearly, he had been thinking about what I said: "You know, Nathan, I didn't mean that I didn't need or want this job, I just mean that I've stayed loyal to this company for a long time and they kind of owe me."

Really?

"Yeah, I've passed on a lot of opportunities I could've taken advantage of and left, and maybe I would have been more successful if I had. But I never did."

I've heard this story before: Despite his charming and funny demeanor, this guy had grown complacent and resentful. Maybe he was once as successful as he could be. Maybe those opportunities were real and he did pass. Maybe he even did it out of his idea of loyalty—the same misguided loyalty that leaders in the middle have for employees like him. But his justification for his loyalty was about fear of what he didn't do, which cost him. It was a fear that those opportunities had now passed him by. He was now stuck in his job without the will to get better.

What this situation inevitably leads to in employees like this one is not just complacency but resentment for those who lead them: A "you owe me" mindset. The belief that "I am important *and* required."

Nobody Is "Owed" Nuthin'

Years ago, as a district sales director, I visited some of the stores in my area with my boss. During our last store visit, he asked the store manager if we could do anything to help him and his team be more successful. The manager looked at us and said, "Sure, we don't always feel the love. So if you and Nathan could show us the love more often that would be great!"

My boss smiled, looked at the manager, and said, "Do you get paid every two weeks? [Manager nods.] Then there you go! You get love every two weeks." My boss wasn't joking or being mean. He just knew that because of his mandated recognition programs (such as consistent forms of gratitude and acknowledgment calls, top performers award programs, coaching efforts, semi-annual "bonding" meetings), there was nothing but love and gratitude going on. That was probably why this was the only manager on all our stops who mentioned this. The manager was not a bad person, but like a spoiled child, he felt that no matter how much money, recognition, or support he was given, it was never going to be enough.

For leaders in the middle, this mindset can be dangerous because it makes those they lead feel resentment and frustration for something they're getting—even getting

abundantly. That's just a small way entitlement breeds resentment after a few months. Now imagine how much resentment might build up after ten years of those feelings,
and then you get what was happening with that engineer.

When employees like the engineer resent their organizations and leaders because they feel they sacrificed themselves for their jobs, they become the employee version of
"loyalty" to a fault. This warped version of loyalty is not a
big problem because of one's actions alone. It's also a problem because of the blame game these employees play. Under the guise of loyalty, they blame the company for their
missed opportunities or perceived lack of "love." Employees
like the engineer who get this way are on autopilot, doing
only what they need to do to stay successful and claim their
paychecks. They make it clear to anyone who will listen that
they are important and required.

All that blame and entitlement almost always takes a
toll on their leaders and their teams if not handled directly,
which was certainly the case with the engineer. The day I
spoke to that employee, I also spoke to his boss. She had
only been with the company for a short time and had inher-
ited the team. She immediately seized on it and appreciated
this engineer's past successes and institutional memory. Of
course, as you now know, that links loyalty to tenure, which
in this case led to not only his feelings of entitlement but his
boss's defense of his actions. "He one of the smartest guys I
have. He knows more about what we do than anyone else,"
she told me. "But he is by far the biggest pain in the ass of
anybody." She stopped herself and thought for a moment before continuing: "He kind of has that right, though."

What do you mean he has that "right"?

"He's very helpful, and the team loves him. He doesn't tend to follow directions and wants to do his own thing, but he's entitled to do his own thing after being here so long. And as long as he is doing his own thing, he is fine. When I try and coach him on anything else, he's difficult to manage."

I see this at every company I've worked with in every department: Employees become so "knowledgeable" about their jobs that their bosses rely on them for that knowledge. Thus, they tolerate everything those people do, not because they're good, but because the leaders fear losing that knowledge and the consistent (but not growing) success that comes with it. In this scenario, everyone is held captive to tenure under the guise of loyalty. It sounds good—even noble—to proclaim loyalty for tenure. But it's just an excuse for not coaching down and serving up.

This engineer believed he had his boss and thus his company over a barrel, and they refused to call his bluff and hold him accountable. And because no one was demanding more of themselves or each other, he was winning the mind game. I tried to explain this to his boss. I laid out what would happen next and probably had started to happen before she took over:

You have ten other people on your team, and you're telling me that this guy is your stud and is also your biggest pain in the ass? And you tolerate it not because of his effort but because of time served and how smart he is? You have a team of engineers! They're all smart. You're eventually going to have ten other smart engineers looking to be the biggest pain in the ass. Because they all want to be like this guy is and feel entitled to the same privileges and loyalty. They're either going to be so good they feel they can tell you what to do, or they are going to leave because they feel less significant and appreciated.

If and when that happens at that company, it's something that can't be solved by coaching the others because they see that coaching as punishment for not being pains in your ass too. Most importantly, that engineer was not serving his boss with his behavior and soon neither will the rest of the team until she holds everyone, regardless of their tenure, accountable. Because no one "owes" anyone loyalty. Loyalty must be earned every day and only lasts as long as the contribution continues and grows.

Six months later the boss of that engineer got a new boss herself—one with a serve up/coach down mindset. In their first one-on-one meeting, the new boss asked her about the engineer, and she told him about all the issues she dealt with and why she continued to put up with his attitude and behaviors. The new boss told her that her team, the organization, and the engineer all deserved better. He coached on how to have the hard conversation with the engineer that he must line up and do more or make a change. When she followed through that week, the engineer decided it was time to move on and find his next adventure.

Six months after the engineer left not only did the team not lose any ground but they are thriving. Morale was at an all-time high. Even better, the engineer found happiness too. He actually thanked his old boss for forcing him to do what he had been afraid to do and make a choice to find a new challenge.

But This Person Sacrificed So Much for the Company!

As we have seen in every part of this book, choices have consequences, and too often, the choice we make is the most comfortable or the one that brings the most immediate gratification. As leaders in the middle, we must *choose* to coach. We must *choose* to serve. These are not the easiest choices, so we must have the will to see those choices through. When leaders are willing to push themselves and those around them to be more and do more and not accept anything less, the pain and fear that leads to inaction goes away and makes everybody's tomorrow better. The engineer did not sacrifice opportunities, he just made a choice not to take them. But when he was pushed, he realized the consequence of that decision and made a new one—the one he should have made years before.

This is why leaders in the middle must coach everyone up or out no matter their time served. That may sound harsh, but is it? Or is it common sense?

If you perceive it as harsh, most likely you were managed, not coached. No one demanded anything from you, and you lost the will to demand anything from your boss *and* yourself. You settled into a mindset of complacency and doing enough to stay successful but never get better.

If you perceive it as common sense, most likely you were coached and understood that no matter your job or title, your commitment is to be and give your best every day.

Of course, there are times when it is hard not to feel the "everyone is important, but no one is required" approach is harsh. Consider the scenario when leaders in the middle have to let long-tenured employees go. Employees say: "I sacrificed my family for this job. I traveled and worked eighty hours a week and now twenty years later, the company that I sacrificed my family for is just going to let me go?" Don't you owe those employees for their loyalty? No. You might owe them a final paycheck and any retirement savings tied to the company, but everything after that—from severance to a send-off party—is a choice. As was the choice of the employee to do what he or she did for twenty years in working for you.

Put it this way: You always hear, "He gave twenty years to that company" but you never hear, "They paid that guy for twenty years of contribution."

Listen, we all want to feel valued and feel that our work and effort has purpose, but when that feeling leads us to resentment or blame, it becomes a fault. This scenario is no different than the engineer's choice I recounted before. These people made the decision to stay at their companies and work eighty hours a week. Whatever the reason was, *they made it.* If people regret it now, it's easier to blame others for that decision to mitigate the sting of being let go than admit the consequences of their actions.

Chances are, these people also knew what they were getting into in the first place. They decided that eighty hours a week was worth it for what it provided for them and their families: status, houses in nice neighborhoods, fancy cars, the latest cell phones and other gadgets, nice vacations . . . Heck, they may have really enjoyed their work too and felt a real sense of pride in their jobs and drive to do better. Then they lost the will to keep doing it. Their families aren't to blame for the decision. Their bosses and their companies aren't either. *They are.*

You don't get to blame your bosses or organizations in hindsight for your decisions and losing your will. You are usually the source of your problems—not your people, bosses, or clients.

This doesn't mean employees and team members are not worthy and don't deserve happiness and success. Everyone deserves happiness and success. It just may or may not be found in your or anyone's current job. Just like no one is required, no job or job title is required either. This is about one's value as a person as much as it is about not allowing anyone to be entitled, complacent, and resentful under the mask of loyalty. People are more than one job or what they do for a living, and no one should wait for what is owed to them. Every opportunity should be sought after and pursued, regardless of who you are, where you work, or how long you have been there.

Serve Up/Coach Down Mindset: Loyalty Versus Tenure

No one is owed anything but a paycheck for services rendered. As soon as we start thinking we are entitled to more, we stop giving more to earn that paycheck! Leaders in the middle must know that no one's job (not even our own) is guaranteed by what we have done. All of us must earn our jobs every day, every week, and every year. Loyalty comes from contribution, not tenure.

The wrong mindset fueled by poor coaching and an inability to serve up: I choose the status quo. I'm disrespecting and being disloyal to long-time employees by expecting them to do more and contribute better after ten or twenty years than they did after one or two. I need to protect these people, because I need them to succeed. If they were to leave, I don't know what I would do. I don't need to coach them. I need to keep them happy. It serves the company well to keep them happy, even if they are pains in the ass.

The correct mindset fueled by great coaching and an ability to serve up: I choose to be better. I must serve my company and my boss first by coaching everyone up or out, regardless of tenure. Serving up means prioritizing the needs of my company first, and I serve them and show appreciation for my team by coaching down to make them better and exceed expectations. In sports, teams draft new players every year, and veterans have to earn their job every year. If we want to build a thriving winning culture, we must commit to doing the same in business.

CHAPTER 22

Choose Wisely: Sacrifice Versus Decision

I spent the first nine years of my professional life working sixty to eighty hours a week for a company I loved. When I started, I did not have kids, and I loved what did so I worked all the time through the weekend. At one point, I was assigned to beautiful Puerto Rico for a few months, but my feet never touched the sand of the island's beaches. I never explored the island. I hung out at the hotel and in town when I wasn't working. But it wasn't a sacrifice. I loved working and was accountable to no one but me. I chose to work those hours.

Today, I have a wife and four kids I love spending time with *and* a job I love to do. That job has me traveling all year long, and I can be gone for two weeks at a time. But I refuse to make the choices I did when I first started out. I'm accountable to them and well as my clients. I'm not sacrificing my family for my career *or* my career for my family. I am choosing to maximize my time in both. Even as I work the hours I do, I will keep taking my youngest daughter fishing, escorting my teenage daughter to her date while listening to her god-awful music, and sitting in a chair (no phone in hand) while my middle daughter reads me the latest book she spent a week writing while I was away. My oldest son is now married and expecting a kid; I will be available anytime he needs parenting advice.

And I need to keep maximizing that time: *Only when we have the commitment to and passion for everything in our lives that are important do we succeed at them. Because nothing is a sacrifice; it's all about the choices we make.*

The same goes for family, friendships, and serving up to your boss and coaching down your to your team. You choose to be the person those people count on. You never want then to expect or accept less. All personal and professional relationships require work to maintain. You need to show up every day. You can't let "time served" be an excuse for not working to make your relationships better.

This is why my wife and I renew our vows every five years. Most parents put their kids in front of each other. Everything is about and for the kids. Not in my family. My wife and I serve each other first. I owe some of this to my wife's grandmother who always told her to serve her husband first, because when your kids leave you, he will be the only one left. But that's not the only reason. I want my girls to see how I treat their mother and my son to see how to be a good husband. And just because I serve my spouse first does not mean I love my kids any less. Plus, when your kids come first, marriage becomes like an obligation—a job without pay.

Why Am I Telling You All This?

Because in this analogy for leaders in the middle, our bosses, organizations, and customers are our "spouses" and the people we lead people are our "kids." Just because you serve your boss and company first does not mean you don't love and appreciate your team. It means you have a job to do and keep doing better and better—and that you have the same expectations for your team: to keep contributing and earning that loyalty day in and day out moving forward. Why would leaders in the middle expect any less from themselves at work and from the people they are leading?

Take a hard look at all your team members right now and ask yourself:

▷ Who on your team are you demanding the most from? Why?

▷ Who are you demanding the least from? Why?

▷ Is the person you are demanding the most from your most tenured employee? Do they call what they are doing a sacrifice?

▷ Do you have the same high expectations (or higher) for the people who have been with the team the longest? Do you have the highest expectations for yourself?

▷ Are the people you are demanding the least from led or held accountable by people who demand the least from themselves and their people? Is that person you?

Remember: Lower-level issues start with upper-level people. Just because employees make choices they later regret or think entitles them to more, doesn't mean leaders in the middle aren't complicit in the problem. Just like lack of accountability, lack of understanding what loyalty means and how it is earned usually goes straight to the top. If leaders in the middle accept subpar results, then they are not only failing to serve up but also will choose to accept even less from the people they are supposed to be coaching—and themselves!

Serve Up/Coach Down Mindset: Sacrifice Versus Decision

Everything we do as a leader in the middle is about choice.

The wrong mindset fueled by poor coaching and an inability to serve up: I sacrifice for my leaders and company; they owe me.

The correct mindset fueled by great coaching and an ability to serve up: I choose to serve my leaders and company. I owe it to them to push myself to get better and coach my team to success.

CHAPTER 23

Dreaming Big to Be Big: Loyalty and High Performance

A young sales rep took a job at a trade show marketing company. After two months on the job learning the ropes and all he could from his bosses and other reps, he told his boss and everyone on the team that he was ready: He will soon be the number-one sales rep in the company and double what the top rep does today. Many of his teammates felt he was what Texans call "all hat and no cattle" (all talk and no action). They called him cocky. But he backed up his words. He managed his time, asked his boss for coaching to serve him and their clients better, made three times the calls of everyone else, and traveled anywhere at any time to meet with prospects.

Sure enough, by his second year, this rep was number one with more than $1.8 million in sales. By his fourth year, he was selling more than $4 million. Today, he does a little more than

$5 million. Now, here's the rub: No one had done more than $2 million when this rep started. These days, that is middle of the pack.

All boats rise with the tide? Nope, it was more than that. Talking to the other reps at the company, they admitted thinking this kid was too full of himself and making empty promises. They called him a suck-up. But when they saw him delivering on those promises, it shook them out of their complacency. This kid wasn't sucking up. He wasn't acting maliciously or undermining them. He wasn't manipulating anyone to get what he wanted. He was just delivering results and exceeding expectations—something other reps hadn't done for years. They had been successful, but only to a point. This kid was a high-performing superstar, and he made everyone around him want to get better and do more to serve their clients and boss. Dismissing him as cocky was simply blaming him for the will they had lost to work hard and demand the same coaching from their boss.

All because this kid knew what every leader in the middle must to serve up and out and coach down: *Before you can win, you need the desire to win. To be big, you need to dream big. You need to go for it!*

Earlier I laid out how some leaders in the middle believe building a bench is disloyal to the team you have. The example of this young rep shows exactly why it is not: He backed his words with actions and built on every success to demand more of himself. He made the entire team *choose* to do better. He didn't have more knowledge or experience than any of the other reps. He just felt he wasn't entitled to anything and pushed himself to act to make his dreams a reality.

In my last book, I wrote about being logical when setting goals. Setting realistic goals is often justification for not dreaming big like those other reps. Realistic goals are limiting because they are realistic; they are based on what one has seen or done before. The young rep set logical goals. He was thinking big, not just dreaming it. Logical means, given the time and the will, I can achieve whatever goal is possible, not just what is realistic.

Leaders in the middle must push themselves and their teams to dream in the biggest ways possible and do the important tasks and activities, even when there are not any immediate results or evidence that the dream is even possible to become reality.

Success in Business Is Built on Successful Moneyships

I probably could have ended this part here and sent you on your way. But after talking so much about misplaced loyalty and self-importance when it comes to understanding what it means to be important but not required, I wanted to go a little deeper about how this young rep delivered big. It went beyond his serve up mindset or his openness to coaching from his boss. Simply put, he served out to his clients and turned those relationships into "moneyships."

I have heard thousands of people say "sales is a relationship business" as if it is *the* hidden secret to success. I agree that sales is a relationship business, but the secret isn't relationships: *The secret to success—and being appreciated and valued by your boss and your organization—is having the mindset to turn all business relationships into "moneyships."*

This relationship principle is for all businesspeople whether you are in sales, HR, finance, customer service, manufacturing, working the floor of a factory . . . and especially for leaders in the middle who want to keep serving up at the highest levels. A strong and genuine relationship with our clients and customers is essential. But that's about communication and rapport. Moneyships are about being valuable to those you do business with to build your business. This has nothing to do with spending money on clients, taking them out to dinner, and sending them gifts. In fact, it's the exact opposite: Turning relationships in to moneyships is about getting others to give you money or do business with you because you are valuable to their success.

Too many leaders forget this. I'm sure many of the reps in that trade show office had. Salespeople and businesspeople in many industries have lots of relationships, but too often those relationships never grow in to moneyships that generate more business or income for the organization they work for. After all, "important but not required" goes for your clients' perception of you too. If you are not important and adding value to them, it doesn't matter how likeable you are. They'll grab a beer with you after they sign a deal with your competitor.

Three Steps to Convert Relationship to Moneyships

1. **Be clear on your intentions.** Never have a hidden agenda but know there is always something in it for you. If your goal is a

long-term relationship to gain your customers' business, then tell them that and *show* them what success looks like. Any business deal is a win-win. If you tell people what you're doing and where you're going, they never have to guess where you're coming from or what your angle is. They already know it.

2. ***Be persistent, bold, and confident.*** You must know that to serve those around us we must make them look good. To do this, you must not be afraid to get to know someone and let them know you. You must be willing to swallow your pride and be vulnerable, especially if you don't have the answers right away. That takes great confidence—and follow-through. No moneyship starts from one conversation. Be ready to ask multiple times, leave multiple messages, and get rejected multiple times.

3. ***Put it all together.*** Align the moneyship with your team's organization. As good a deal as it might be, you serve the people who pay you first. Any deal must be a flawless experience for them too.

Many leaders in the middle with whom I share these steps agree with them, but they and their teams fall way short on the actual execution. That's because when it comes to putting it all together, they forget about coaching down while serving up and out. Each of these steps is coachable through scrimmages, practice meetings, one-on-ones, and ride days. You know, the important tasks we forget to manage our time to do. Like I said before, the consequences of not doing them aren't immediate, but they will be felt in the long term. Especially when someone like that young rep takes that business away.

Final Considerations: Everyone Is Important, but No One Is Required

Yes, the answer to these questions is all the same.

Are you confusing loyalty and accountability? Serve up by holding yourself and your people accountable to their results and exceeding expectations today, and demand everyone continue to get better in the future. Coach them up or out!

Are you confusing loyalty with tenure? Serve up by holding yourself and your people accountable to their results and exceeding expectations today, and demand everyone continue to get better in the future. Coach them up or out!

Are you being loyal to your top performers and leveraging their successes so everyone dreams big? Serve up by holding yourself and your people accountable to their results and exceeding expectations today, and demand everyone continue to get better in the future. Coach them up or out!

PART 7

Keeping the Power

At the start of this book, I said that too many people leading from the middle think their position is weak and lacks influence. These people tell me they struggle to convey any power or authority when "everyone knows" they have a boss that is making the "real decisions." And you know what? They're right! Those people leading from the middle are *middle managers*, not *leaders in the middle*. That feeling of powerlessness those managers have doesn't come from the fact that they're in the middle. Middle managers lack power because they give it all away.

Leaders in the middle who serve up and coach down *own* their power. That's the single difference between middle management and leading from the middle: power. But once you own that power, how do you keep it? The first part of the answer is the same as what got you to this point: You choose to own it. Your power is completely yours to own or give away. The second part of the answer to keeping the power is you must execute that decision by mastering all the issues covered in this book.

CHAPTER 24

Own Your Power

Sitting in our weekly leadership meeting, the other regional directors and I sensed something was different. My boss had been frustrated for months with the directions and decisions our company was making, and his lack of control of and ability to make decisions affecting that direction. This week, as he tried to explain the next steps we would take, we asked our usual round of questions to understand how things would work, and his frustration bubbled over: "Guys, I don't have the power to make decisions. They do. All I am is a highly paid sales rep."

You have to understand my boss was not a bad leader. In fact, up to that moment, he was one the best I had worked with in my career. But with those words, he lost his power as an effective leader. Not because of the company's decision, rather, it was his words and ensuing actions that took his power. He lost his influence as a leader in the middle and became a middle manager. He showed up, but he didn't lead. Instead of serving his bosses by owning the direction and our responsibility as a team to implement it, he blamed the company for his lack of influence. He told us that he didn't like the direction and complained to us about it. He stopped working with us on how to implement the changes and holding us accountable to get better results from them. He then made excuses to his boss for our results, protecting up instead of serving up. In other words, my boss stopped serving up and coaching down.

By this point in the book, you know that *claiming* power as leaders in the middle is about having that serve up/coach down mindset. *Owning* the power is about executing the important tasks of coaching and serving:

▷ Understanding that titles are irrelevant to power. Our power comes from how we make our bosses look good and how we impact and influence our teams by coaching them.

▷ Following every direction as if it were our own direction and making sure our teams do the same—whether we think it is right or wrong, we believe!

▷ Demanding accountability and results from yourself and team to serve out to your customers as well as our bosses, refusing to accept any excuses or to blame our bosses or the company for our problems.

Keeping the power as a leader in the middle is about sustaining the execution of coaching and serving, never wavering in the face of challenges and changes (regardless of what you think of them) and always—*always*—working to get better and exceed expectations. My old boss showed how challenging that can be. His ego and words got in his way, and he never recovered his leader-in-the-middle serve up/coach down mindset.

Within a year, he walked out of a job he talked himself out of months before. All because he did not understand this essential principle of keeping the power: *Leading from the middle is a powerful choice. Once you have that power, it is yours to wield; no one can take it from you. You sustain your power by constantly and consistently serving up and coaching down.*

Own the Direction

Every one of us will face the situation my boss did in their careers, where we feel just like a cog in a wheel, forced to buy in to one more directive. But we only become that cog when we act like one. It's a fantasy to think that everyone will agree with every decision their company or boss makes. And as we discussed earlier in this book, the best leaders and companies don't want "yes people" who blindly follow every direction given. They want "how people" who ask questions to understand and challenge themselves to do more in order to buy in and execute.

My boss forgot how to do that, which was his choice. Because it certainly wasn't me or the other directors who made that choice. As I said, he was one of the best bosses I ever had, and most of the directors felt the same way. He just gave up his power that day by making himself powerless in our eyes.

What could my boss have done in this scenario? Let's play it out as if things happened a little differently. Say my boss didn't have his problem, the directors did. After another change to the company's marketing platform, we didn't know what to think anymore. Despite our boss's unwavering belief, direction, and coaching, we were becoming discouraged, feeling like we had little power—like cogs in a wheel. So at that weekly meeting, it was us instead of our boss who called ourselves "glorified sales reps." How would you react if you were our boss?

Before you answer, know that actually happened at my company. When our new boss arrived, morale had been low and some of us had adopted the same attitude our old boss had. She asked us if we had felt our old boss really had been just a glorified sales rep. "No," we all said. "Until that day, we felt he made the decisions." Our new boss called us on that:

> You're only half right. He did have all the power, but he didn't make all the decisions. No one does. And the only reason he lost that power is because he chose to give it away, just like you are doing now. Power comes from ownership, and ownership does not require that one actually make the decision. It only requires that one owns the direction and execution.

It was a lesson I never forgot: *Own the direction and decisions of your boss and company, and direct your team as if they were your own.*

It's Never "Us" Versus "Them"

What could my old boss have done to keep the power when faced with his situation was to remember there is no "he" or "she" or "them" when leading from the middle. Leaders in the middle may never create the direction, but we always own it and the execution. There is only "I" and "we" and "us." Anything else is blaming others, sometimes accidentally. For example, in trying to sympathize with our followers, a leader in the middle might say, "I don't agree with this direction, but it's what the company wants us to do." That simple statement blames the company and undermines a leader's power to demand accountability. Or say leaders tell their people that they "will be the voice of the team and let those in power know how their decisions are negatively affecting us." That "us versus them" mindset puts the leader in a position of "messenger," and no messenger I know had ever been in a position of power.

Again, it is essential to remember that "owning" still gives leaders in the middle license to seek and ask questions to understand the decision or the task to get our team aligned with the goals. Once they do, they share it with their team by saying, "Here is what we are going to do" or "The reason this is important to us is . . ." or "Our job is to implement this plan and execute it to maximize our success." If a team member asks, "Who's idea is this?" the leader should respond genuinely and passionately, "Yours, mine, and ours! The company has the data and vision to know this is the right direction for all of us. Our job is make sure our leaders know we are the right team to achieve it."

The problem is when we believe there is an "us" and a "them" but proclaim otherwise. Then our words betray our mindset and undermine our power *and* our authenticity.

Power Is Not Reclaimed or Shown by Force

Steve Martin once described what happens when we go to a foreign country, get in a taxi, ask to go to our hotel, and find out the driver does not speak English. Our first instinct is to speak louder: "I WOULD LIKE TO GO TO THE HOTEL"—as if being more forceful will suddenly trigger latent language synapses in the driver and compel him to magically understand. It never works. And it doesn't work in business either. If you don't believe in and own the direction your company is going, then forcing people to "do it or else" will not make you more believable or restore your power. Power does not come from force. In fact, being powerful as a leader in the middle requires humility and confidence to sustain mastery of all the issues we confronted in this book.

▷ Power is shown by being the leader in the middle a boss can count on to serve up and coach down, no matter what.

▷ Power comes from accountability and genuine ownership of every direction during times of uncertainty—so much so your team will follow even if they think you might have lost your mind.

▷ Power means making the time for the important tasks of coaching and developing your team and not using the excuse that "they should know this already." Because no one knows all the answers, including you.

▷ Power is mandating that new knowledge get implemented and following through to make sure it does.

▷ Power is confronting employees that are not doing their best and coach them up or out, not because you're the boss but because those employees deserve more and so does the team.

Simply put, how you serve up and coach down is going to determine how you keep the power as a leader in the middle—or don't. I have found when leaders in the middle demonstrate that kind of power, their bosses give them more power and their people push themselves to serve them. You don't just keep the power; they want to keep you *in* power.

Serve Up/Coach Down Mindset: Own Your Power

You don't need an *S* on your chest to claim, own, and keep the power you have as a leader in the middle. It is ours to keep by serving up and coaching down, and ours to give away by failing to own the direction and decisions of our bosses and the company.

The wrong mindset fueled by poor coaching and an inability to serve up: Saying to your team that "they" are making us do XYZ and blaming the company and your bosses for the decision. Making excuses when you and your team get complacent and fail to deliver the best results, because it was obviously a bad decision to begin with.

The correct mindset fueled by great coaching and an ability to serve up: Your power is yours to own. You are always the boss of your team. Your power is not in your title. It's in your mindset and your actions. You have the same high standards for those you lead and refuse to accept excuses or make excuses to those you serve.

CHAPTER 25

The Power Is in the Goal, Not Being Right

One day I was using my GPS to find a store and drove right past it. As I did, my daughter mustered her best parental mocking tone and said, "Dad, you just missed the store." But I never saw it, because my GPS didn't say, "You have arrived at your destination." You've probably had this happen to you. Maybe you've even heard of more dramatic versions of this like a person driving into a lake because his GPS told him to keep going. On the real roads of life, those people are probably crazy—or just stupid for not using their eyes. On the proverbial roads of business, however, these are the best leaders in the middle to have on your team because their company and bosses are the GPS, and they owned the direction they were given.

That GPS analogy is perfect for what a leader in the middle must do to keep the power by serving in uncertain times: Believe in the direction and own it, even if you think it might be wrong or possibly crazy. Everything we have discussed in this book is all about setting up leaders in the middle to keep the power by achieving the results demanded of them by owning that responsibility without challenging the direction.

But They're Wrong!

When a company shifts direction for the future, leaders in the middle must believe it is for the best. Of course, there is no evidence the company is right. They just made a decision based on its vision and all available evidence. One would believe the people at the top have a longer view and more evidence than people in the middle and the bottom to make those decisions.

So why question it? Because *you* think you're right? That's just ego talking, and it is a surefire way for leaders in the middle to lose their power in uncertain times, because *keeping the power doesn't have anything to do with being right.*

What do you do when the evidence tells you otherwise? Drive into the lake. Yes, drive into the lake. If that's what you have been told to do, you execute. Go ahead and question to understand: *How would you drive on this lake, boss? Anything I should know to make this turn into a James Bond car?* I'm not doubting the direction; I'm checking to make sure we're aligned, not because I'm thinking we're going to drown. What happens when you do? Sometimes your boss might say, "Whoa, there's a lake?! Stop! That wasn't there when we planned this." Sometimes your boss might say, "Wait, you're supposed to take a left there. Thanks for checking in. That could have cost us." But most of the time? Your boss is going to say, "Yup, keep going. Great job." Not because he is a bad human or not paying attention but because he owns the direction given to him and needs you to own it for yourself and your team too.

So how many of you would drive into the lake? Too many people leading from the middle don't. One of the biggest weaknesses of leaders in the middle is that they want to be right—or rather, to not be wrong. They'd actually rather be right and fail than wrong and succeed. Instead of executing at the highest levels, they do as little as possible to avoid consequences and use that mindset to justify not holding themselves and their people accountable.

We sacrifice so much for being right, but *why?* Being right is not power. There is a difference between being right and doing the right thing. You must continue to serve up. Never blame those you serve for decisions you do not agree with. Remember: There is no "us and them," just "us," and we need to find a way to get through that lake. Fight through the fear and doubt, and do it. Besides, when times are uncertain, there may not even be a lake. You just *think* you see one. And what happens if you do drown, your team looking at you as you sink to the bottom and fail? So be it. You failed with all you had and most leaders will tell you that only leads to greater success along the way.

I would rather fail doing the right thing, serving up, then get fired for failing to keep my power and execute—and challenging my people to do the same to achieve more.

The Power Is in the Goal

I was working with a client on setting management expectations and goals for the next year when my client started to balk.

"Nathan, we have to be careful. Our goals are higher this year. In fact, they are 25 percent higher than last year's goals. Some leaders are going to have huge push back."

Wow! Twenty-five percent more than what you did this year?

"No, 25 percent higher than last year's goal. It's only 90 percent of what we actually did this year."

I started to laugh. Now I know it is easy to laugh when it's not your goal, but you can't call a number a goal if you have already achieved it! A goal is something you should have to strive to achieve, not be the same as you have done (or less than) before. Sure, there are exceptions to that rule, but generally, this client's "goal" was an acceptance of defeat.

Why are you setting a goal that is only 90 percent of this year's?

"Because the goals affect people's bonuses."

I used to be a leader like my client. I would negotiate the lowest goal possible to set compensation in the team's favor. Then I would tell my team that we were going to kill it and make some good bonuses. It works. Until it doesn't. Slowly but surely, in spite of the big bonuses, you give your power away by failing to set realistic achievement goals and raising expectations year over year. You get complacent. You stop coaching and demanding more, which is what happened to me before I shifted my mindset to serving up and coaching down and made my team three promises when it came to goals and expectations:

1. Every year, I am going to raise your goal.
2. You will always have to deliver more results to make the same amount of money.
3. Work smart and you will always make more money and have more success than the previous year.

Twenty years later, I found myself sharing that story with my client, and he understood. He owned my promises, shared them with his team, and changed his goal to a 25 percent increase overall. Needless to say, the team is well on their way to crushing these numbers and helping their boss keep the power. Because keeping the power is not just about owning the direction of our bosses. It has as much to do with challenging our teams with goals that drive more power instead of lowering expectations to match lower results and accepting less.

When leaders lower goals, the short-term benefit of bigger bonuses that leads to cash-infused morale hides the larger issue: As leaders, we now have sent the message that whenever we feel a goal is unreachable, we take the power of reaching higher away from our employees. I believe to be the best leaders in the middle, *we must believe that our team can hit any logical goal because that says we all have the power to do what we believe.*

I understand that this might affect some incomes and livelihoods in the short run, but it also drives us to do more. That should be the case any time we miss our goals. If our kids don't get an *A* on a test, we don't ask the teacher to change the test next time. We tell our kids to study harder, better, or differently. We tell them they are missing the goal because they are not doing enough of something or they need to modify or change their behavior

The point is: *Don't lower the goal; own the miss.* The best leaders in the middle do.

They know power is given to those who give, deliver, and demand great effort, desire, and commitment to winning. And they are always proven right.

Serve Up/Coach Down Mindset: The Power Is in the Goal, Not Being Right

We lead with the power we have. It doesn't matter about the limits or how little we have. It doesn't matter how difficult the competition is or what market we are in. It is all about where we end up and not where we had to come from to keep the power. Our success becomes the journey we are on.

The wrong mindset fueled by poor coaching and an inability to serve up: Screw my boss and company; I'm not driving into the lake! I'm not going down for this idea. It's not my decision. I'll stop and do just enough to keep my job and not kill myself for it. I'd rather lower my expectations and exceed those goals than push myself to do more. I'd rather be comfortable doing less.

The correct mindset fueled by great coaching and an ability to serve up: My power comes from my belief, and my belief drives my team's belief. The organization expects us to achieve this goal, and if that means driving into the lake, so be it! We must never lower our goals to match our results. We must raise our efforts to make our results match our goals. Real success is not in the result. Real success is in the fight along the way.

CHAPTER 26

It's Never "Me Versus the World"

"He's coming to our quarterly meeting!" My coaching client was clearly deeply concerned at the prospect of this mysterious intruder's invasion.

Who is?

"My boss!"

I shouldn't have been surprised, but every time a leader in the middle tells me this (and it happens all the time), I am. It didn't matter that this client was one of my best students and the quarterly meeting was just an extension of the work he was doing with his team. He had become a strong leader in the middle and embraced his power. He had been doing his weekly one-on-ones consistently for months and set clear expectations that challenged his team to deliver bigger results. His people had scrimmaged important client meetings and pitches. That said, he had also learned to serve up, delivering a weekly dashboard report of all the team's activities and results to his boss. And yet he was still borderline freaked out at the prospect of that boss coming to the meeting.

Why are you so concerned about this?

"Because my boss will challenge everything my people are doing and make them feel frustrated and defensive. He will take over the meeting and take us off agenda, making the meeting less effective."

I knew this client's boss well. There was a good chance he was right about what would happen. But here's the rub: My client might have felt that way even if he didn't have a boss like that. Too many leaders in the middle who have done everything to claim, own, and keep their power by coaching down and serving up still hate having the boss come to their meetings. As open as they have become, they would still like to keep the door to the conference room and office closed. Because they perceived that open door or seat at the table as a threat to their power.

It's not, and it's the last hurdle to serving and coaching I need you to clear: Leaders in the middle must welcome everyone to the table. Sharing time and space with others is how we demonstrate, not that we have power, but that we are secure in our ownership of it.

No One Wants to Be a Guest in Their Own House

As leaders in the middle, we must welcome the chance for our boss, our boss's boss, or anyone they deem important to join our team and meetings at any time. Let them see the powerful work you're doing. What have you got to hide?

Don't let fear and doubt undermine what you have achieved by serving up. Even if you do get challenged or questioned, this does not make you less powerful unless you allow it to and give your power away to your boss. Besides, you are part of *his* coaching team too. Every sports team has a bunch of assistant coaches who answer to the head coach. The head coach does not have to tiptoe around the assistant coaches, and the assistant coaches don't avoid the head coach or make him feel unwelcome. "No coach in sports and no boss in his business should feel like guests in their house," meaning no leader should feel like they have to ask permission to engage in a team's meeting.

Again, it's not just weak managers who see this as a threat. Many leaders in the middle—even those who serve up—can get a little "me versus the world" mindset when the boss comes calling. They start thinking their teams need protection (they don't) and that it's a referendum on their leadership (it's not). So here's a novel approach to losing that mindset and putting your fears and doubts to bed: *Talk to your boss!*

▷ Make sure that your boss knows you are excited about his or her participation as this is your boss's team too, not just yours.

▷ Share your expectations and thoughts and ask your boss to share his or hers.

▷ Let your boss know what your goal is and any concerns you may have about the team misunderstanding his or her position or how they might be intimidated by his or her presence.

That's what I told my client that day: We are one team with one agenda. It's never you against anyone. And you know what? The meeting went "fine, great even." My client followed my advice and laid out a clear plan for his boss's participation. His boss is real hard-nosed, and although he never strayed from the agenda, he challenged my client and his team. But they responded without any defensiveness. In fact, they were happy to meet the challenge because they were proud of what they had achieved, and it showed in their results and their morale.

When You Keep Your Power, You Welcome Others in Your "Sandbox"

You're not threatened and silo-ed. You aren't territorial because you own who you are and what you do. You own the responsibility for the execution and hold your team accountable to the success of that execution. Never blaming or disbelieving those you serve. Never accepting excuses from those you coach—just owning the results of your team. Why would any boss fight the power of that leader unless he were doing all those things and felt threatened? This is why so many leaders shut the door to others.

But open doors don't reduce your power as a leader in the middle; they enhance it and empower others. Believe me, I know from where I speak. One time, as a regional director, I shared the same office with my managers *and* my boss. That's right, three layers of leadership in one open room. If employees wanted to see a manager and talk about me, they had to do it with me sitting right there. I couldn't have cared less. As a strong, secure leader in the middle, I never feared anyone going to my boss. And neither should you.

That's my advice to you: *Stay open!* Don't let your insecurities get in the way of the power you have. Don't just open the door to your power, dare people to walk in. Face whatever might be out there with confidence. Don't worry if you don't have all the answers. No one does, or expects you to.

As leaders in the middle, we must remember to enjoy the ride and celebrate the power that we have—and the power we give others! That comes from encouraging everyone to open their doors (or wave them into their cubicles) and mean it. Success comes from creating spaces that allow people to express themselves without fear of being "exposed" or judged so you and they can gain insights. Our success and our power are only heightened when we made this journey in the middle together!

Final Considerations: Keeping the Power

Every aspect of a leader in the middle's job—every action taken—has the ability to keep or give away that leader's power. A serve up/coach down mindset supports the activities that allow leaders in the middle to claim, own, and keep the power. That power is about more than a title, more than being the boss.

The true power of leaders in the middle is getting those we lead to achieve results beyond what they believe they could achieve and showing those we serve that we will go beyond our job and their expectations to deliver success.

We will do what it takes. No goal is unrealistic or illogical if we believe in it: There is no lake!

There is no "they" or "them" to blame. We must never separate ourselves or our teams from our leaders. We have a responsibility to carry and sometimes create direction, but regardless, we own it. No excuses. Point your finger at someone else for your problems and you're not just a cog in the wheel. You've allowed yourself to be weak. Because you chose to give away your power.

Commit to Personal Growth

I have snowboarded for more than fifteen years, but every year, my wife and I take a private snowboarding lesson before we hit the slopes. Doesn't matter where we are or who we're with, we do it. One year, a friend who joined us on one of our trips and just wanted to get on the mountain gave us a hard time about the lesson. "I thought you guys knew how to snowboard!" he laughed. Then he mocked us with remarks about how he didn't need or have enough time to take "no stinking lessons." He only had three days to board. We didn't take the bait.

"Good for you," I said. "But the reason we take lessons every year isn't because we don't remember how. It's that no matter how good we are today, we still try to get better every year. We only get to go snowboarding a few times or more a season. The kid giving us lessons is out here every day, all season long. He's a ton better than us, so we can always count on teachers like him making us a little better every year. We think taking a little time to learn and get better is more of a priority than how many trips down the hill we take."

If you're thinking, "Nice story, Nathan, but what the hell do snowboarding lessons have to do with leading from the middle?" The answer is: Actually, a lot. Many leaders in the middle today are like my friend. They feel they are good enough already and don't *need* to get better, so they don't focus on learning or improving. Even if they want to learn and improve, they don't feel they have time to do it.

And even if they made the time, they doubt they could get what they need from someone who might be "beneath" them.

Simply put, don't be like my friend. *Make the time to improve and at least agree to listen to anyone who has experience that you don't. We owe it to ourselves, our families, the people we lead, and those who pay us to be our best.*

I used to be my friend. I had no time for things like this book. Then a mentor of mine asked me if I read books. I answered honestly and told him I didn't, but I did read articles about the industry I worked in, so I was aware of what is going on. He said, "If you want to grow in your career, you must start learning to be better versus learning to be aware." This remains some of the greatest advice I have ever received. I also heard it more and more over the years. Some of the most successful people in the world tell us to read anything and everything, whether it be on business and self-improvement, love and marriage, wealth and prosperity, expanding your mind and mindset—anything that is new and different and that allows for contemplation and learning. What's more, these people back it up. According to "Reading Habits of the Most Successful Leaders that Can Change Your Life Too" by Marissa Levin (*Inc. Magazine,* August 13, 2017):

▷ Warren Buffet reads 500 pages per day.

▷ Mark Cuban reads three hours per day.

▷ Bill Gates reads fifty books per year.

Most successful CEOs I know read on average one book per week. The average American reads less than one per *year.* Yet according to a survey by National Endowment for the Arts, 43 percent of the adults in the United States don't read anything not required by work or school. I refuse to be those people. Today, I read countless books by all kinds of people (even people I don't agree with). I believe so much in the power of books, I have written five of them myself. Okay, truth be told I still don't enjoy reading, but I listen to audio books every day. Because I believe in their power to help me develop and grow as a person and be the best version of me. That's what drives me and keeps me motivated.

Personal development is about having the humility to know we can be better and the discipline to make time for it today. So this is my final challenge to you: *Be the best version of you that you can be today, and be a better version next year. Learn more, read more, and commit to your own personal development so you can coach others to do the same and serve others to the best of your abilities.*

Be Your Best

One morning, I was driving my tenth-grade daughter to school and decided to lay down some words of wisdom about how she must always be learning how to get better at what she does. I don't know exactly how I said it or what it was in response to, but I am sure it was deep, important, and perfectly appropriate for seven o'clock in the morning. Have you felt someone looking at you but at the same time right through you and not listening to anything you say? Now multiply that effect by ten. My daughter had the absolute "I couldn't care less" look on her face as I spoke and when I was done rolled her eyes several times. I decided to validate my value and knowledge by letting her know that business leaders and organizations pay me thousands of dollars to hear my expert advice and insights.

"Dad," she replied. "I would pay for you not to give me your advice or insight." Then she smirked and put on her headphones.

Full disclosure, if this wasn't patently obvious, my kids don't listen to me. I hope you will. Wisdom comes with age and experience. And even though my daughter has perfected the thousand-yard stare, I remain committed to her seeing all the things her mom and I do to ensure our success as a family, especially treating others with love and respect. I want her to see the things I do every day—from listening to specific music that gets me pumped in the morning to reciting from a great business book (*Think and Grow Rich*) to attending a church I believe in to giving and serving others to putting her mom first—all to make myself a better person on an everyday basis.

Because what I want for her (and me) is what I want for you as leaders in the middle: to keep growing. There is an old saying that every living thing is either growing or dying. The same is true in business. It's not enough to be learning about what we are. We must learn how to be better leaders—better people! The greatest leaders in business are the ones still learning and developing within and *beyond* their jobs. They don't like the feeling of being just good enough. They want to be better and challenge how they do things today to how to do them better tomorrow. That means finding the time and making a genuine and committed effort to listen, coach, and be coached—and read! Don't be the "average" American:

▷ **For yourself:** If a physical book scares you, start by spending a minimum of thirty minutes a day "reading" texts that make you think, such as e-books, audio books, TED Talks, podcasts, documentaries. . . Then push to make that an hour.

▷ **For your team:** Mandate that your team spend time growing the same way. Demand that they put it on their calendars so you can see it (even if it means seeing that it is there before they get to the office). If they don't know where to start, recommend what you read and like or feel challenged by.

▷ **For each other:** Use the time during one-on-ones to discuss what they are reading or listening to and have them teach you and their peers what they learned.

I know that's a lot to ask and balance, which is why being a leader in the middle today is one of the most difficult
jobs in business. But it's the only way to avoid one of the
biggest dangers to any leader in any business in any industry: complacency.

Complacency Versus Contentment

Complacency is a mindset that any and all of us can fall victim to. It, like most things in our lives, is not a stage of life
or business. Rather, it is a negative result based on a leader's
loss of will to get better and a decision to stop growing. As
we learned in Part 6: Everyone Is Important, but No One Is
Required, it happens most commonly after we have been
doing a job or working for a company for a long period of
time and find our daily routines boring or no longer challenging. Complacency is the sworn enemy of serving up
and coaching down, because no one who is complacent will
ever commit to making the time, let alone the effort, for the
important tasks of serving and coaching. If a leader says,
"My people are already good enough and know their jobs,
so there is nothing to teach them," then that leader has been
infected by complacency—and it's contagious. Soon their
employees will become complacent too, causing bad morale, unwanted turnover, and of course, poor results.

The opposite is also true. Those leaders in the middle
who make the time to serve up and coach down rarely grow
complacent. There's no time! There is always something to
learn and challenge us to make our employees better and
our bosses look good. If we are reading books, attending workshops on how to do our jobs better, building our

benches, listening to learn, and doing what we need to do to bridge the knowledge gap and implement what we learn, we are doing something new every day to make ourselves and our employees better. This desire to grow is as contagious as the complacency it keeps at bay, leading to an energized culture, people wanting to work for us, and of course, results that regularly exceed expectations.

Complacency is sometimes confused with being content, but they are diametrically opposed. Being content is based on self-gratitude. By being grateful for where I am in my life, I feel content but never complacent. In fact, when I look back to when I left corporate America to become an author, consultant, and motivational speaker, I am genuinely shocked at how blessed I have been to achieve my goals. It took a lot of blind faith, optimism, a ton of activity, and even more mistakes to learn from.

I would bet most of you reading this book feel the same way about your own careers. Look back at who you were when you started, what you have learned, how you have grown, and who you are today. Are you amazed at how your life has changed and grateful for your current success? Then you are content! If you are all those things and also think you're close to being done learning and growing, then you are complacent. Being content still means I get up every morning knowing I'm destined for so much more. I know in my heart that what I will achieve in the next ten years will make today seem small by comparison. I remain thankful and happy with who I am and what I'm doing today but will never lose my ambition to want more for myself and others.

Leaders in the middle must always do the same: *Work on staying content but never complacent—and do the same for those you coach. Remember: The problems at the bottom start with the problems at the top.*

What Are You Waiting For? Put These Words into Action!

Not sure where to start with all this personal growth and development as you lead from the middle? Start with where you live and how you look. The way you and your home looks reflect how you feel about yourself. Do you have the will to work on you? As the flight attendant says, put your oxygen mask on first before helping others.

For example, I don't like to work out or eat healthy, but I know it is important to my wife and essential if I want to stay in shape for my family and be around when my kids have kids. Actually, as I write this book I'm about to become a grandfather! I want to be able to do all the things with all my grandkids that I did with my own kids. I want to see my daughters grow into awesome women just like my son is becoming an awesome man.

Self-care comes in many forms and sizes: spiritual work/prayer, meditation, exercise, eating well, taking time to sleep and rest properly, and getting involved in your community. When we run at full throttle in frenzied caffeine-driven states, we shortchange ourselves and fail to operate at our best. Think of any top-performing leader you know—I mean *top*. Business is booming. Relationships are solid and joyful. Attitude is driven but also peaceful. Are they relatively fit, heath-conscious individuals? Yes, they are. It's absolutely impossible to perform your best if you are not properly caring for your mind and body. That's why I dedicate at least thirty minutes each morning to spiritual tuning, reading, writing, and praying, and at least sixty minutes a day to exercise. Some of this is so my wife won't look at other men, and I don't embarrass myself in swim trunks and shame the other dads. But whatever my motivation, it's making me feel better.

Here is the thing: Don't just think about all these things regarding personal growth and self-care—or write out a *"plan* to do it"—*do* it! Right now. Put down this book and go do something about it. Feeling overwhelmed about where to start? Call your spouse, best friend, or kids. Ask your boss what areas he or she thinks you need to improve on to grow or the places they find personal growth. When you hear something that resonates with you, go do it! Then when you get back, create a personal development and self-care schedule. If you already have one, ask yourself what you can do to make it better.

Most of the time, continued learning, personal development, and self-care does not require additional time. It just requires better management of the time you currently use. Turn your drive time, getting ready time, or waiting time into learning and/or self-care time. Get up twenty-five minutes earlier than usual and use that time to conduct ten minutes of self-care to stretch, ten minutes for reading, and five minutes for writing out goals. It's that simple, and it adds up: Those twenty-five minutes over the course of a year add up to more than one hundred hours of personal development and self-care—and that's only Monday to Friday. Every day you find ways to be more disciplined, more motivated, and more driven, you're doing more than taking care of yourself. You're making sure you are the best version of yourself for the people you love—and others who depend on you as a leader in the middle.